FRUIT PUNCH

ALSO BY KENDRA ALLEN

The Collection Plate

When You Learn the Alphabet

FRUIT PUNCH

A MEMOIR

KENDRA ALLEN

ecco

An Imprint of HarperCollinsPublishers

FRUIT PUNCH. Copyright © 2022 by Kendra Allen. All rights reserved. Printed in
the United States of America. No part of this book may be used or reproduced
in any manner whatsoever without written permission except in the case of
brief quotations embodied in critical articles and reviews. For information,
address HarperCollins Publishers, 195 Broadway, New York, NY 10007.

HarperCollins books may be purchased for educational, business, or sales pro-
motional use. For information, please email the Special Markets Department
at SPsales@harpercollins.com.

Ecco® and HarperCollins® are trademarks of HarperCollins Publishers.

FIRST EDITION

Designed by Michelle Crowe

Library of Congress Cataloging-in-Publication Data has been applied for.

ISBN 978-0-06-304853-9

22 23 24 25 26   LSC   10 9 8 7 6 5 4 3 2 1

For Brooklyn, Riley, and Chloe.

Whenever y'all ready.

All the girls who saw it, changed. I surprised by the ambition
of the unzip. How his face held no shame,

how the way the girls talked I thought they wanted to be
the penis rather than the hand.

—NABILA LOVELACE

I knew you wasn't normal ever since the age of nine.

—DENZEL CURRY

CONTENTS

PART I

BLOOD

PART II

BLOOD

AUTHOR'S NOTE

BEFORE YOU READ THIS BOOK, know that you don't gotta finish it. There's a lot of laughs here (at least I hope), and a lot of memories; but there's also sexual assault, suicidal ideation, physical and emotional violence, and blood. I know we tend to use words like *trigger* and *trauma* loosely, but you know what you know and what you feel, so when you know what it is you're feeling—don't force yourself to sit in my memories with me if it causes even a little bit of suffering. Please put yourself first. Always. & thank you, thank you, thank you for even having *Fruit Punch* in your hands in the first place.

—KENDRA

PRICHARD LANE

JUAN PULLING OUT HIS PENIS is the first time I ever see one. I ain't that good at aligning time with memory, so it all happens around the same age in my head. I'm no older than six. Usually, I'm twelve. Mostly nine. I coulda been four. Iono. Everything's interchangeable. But I know places, and I know we still living on Prichard Lane, which means my parents still live together which mean soon, they won't be. But for now our house is a three-bed/two-bath and I got my own room. The biggest room I ever had to date, prolly cause it's the nineties and Texas rent is cheaper than it's ever been.

Juan's house is to the right of ours and his family don't speak no English so we forced to believe whatever it is he say they said—like we can come over to see his tree house. I don't know nothing bout actual tree houses existing outside of cartoons, let alone in the middle of Pleasant Grove, but Juan real proud of it cause his daddy built it especially for him. My daddy—Doll—be building stuff too. But not no home for his kid.

mostly:	maybe:
cages,	rosters,
walls,	borders,
shelves,	headgear,

Anyways. Juan nem got a pecan tree I like to stand under. It hang over they wooden fence into our front yard and I plant my feet in the grass with a plastic grocery sack looped between my fingers while Doll shake the neck of its limbs. I capture the nuts outta the blades one by one, same way I snatch dandelions outta the earth. When my bag get too heavy to hold, I go sit on our porch's middle step. We got a nice porch. Not the wraparound kind my mama L.A. been dreaming of since she was a lil girl watching TV with too many families with picket fences, but it's nice because its size makes sense.

Doll sit at the top step and hand me one of them metal crackers he took out one of them restaurants we go to when you cracking crab legs open all over the table, but I barely use it. That's what I got a mouth for. I use my baby teeth to pop the pecan shells perfectly. I learn how to do it so fast I obsess over keeping up with the rhythm. It go: Bite. Crack. Pull apart. Chew. Throw. Eat. Repeat. Sometimes I move too fast and fail

to check the quality

of the shell before I consume it, and that be the worst day ever cause a rotten taste immediately swarms across the insides of my jaw. I let my tongue loose; let it all fall out from the back of my throat and cough; like I'm born knowing how to spit things out quick and move on. Pecan shells. Sunflower seeds. People.

L.A. say I act like this because I got a takeover spirit and got a problem with organizing and orchestrating how everybody gotta spend they time in my presence. That I can't handle somebody not liking what I love without shutting down. How it makes me think something is wrong with myself. That I spend too much time—specifically—tryna tell her what I don't wanna do when she the parent.

I'm not tryna have a takeover spirit on purpose; it's just I can't stand people suggesting what it is I need to do in general, let alone with my time. I need room to determine *how* I wanna do the things I'm told. *How* I wanna go about cleaning my room. *How* I wanna dress today. I need time to figure out *how* I can curate the same results in a way that's pleasing to my personality. Something in my brain be telling me to do it slightly differently, slightly wrong, and long, and lonely. To take my time on all tasks asked of me until I get it right. L.A. say not doing what you told—not listening—can get you hurt or get you hit. But I been both a lot of times and ain't die so I don't think it's that big of a deal.

It's prolly why even though L.A. make the best pecan pies—I never save her none in my sack. I eat 'em all and I swipe at my tongue with my fingers once I come across a bad one. I drag what's chewed up along the edge of the concrete step, sit and stare out into the main street at the curb, grab another pecan, hold it up, see if the darkness means sweet or burnt, then start my rhythm back up—slowing it down only to check my work. I study it from all angles so I don't get surprised. I don't understand how this keep getting misinterpreted as disrespectful, or disobedient.

Disobedient is L.A.'s favorite word to define children. She even write it on a piece of construction paper and pin it up on the living room wall with the rest of the words I'm learning to spell like *like*, *space*, and *leave*. Sometimes she even make me use the words in a sentence; like if she lose something in our space, she gone say somebody stole it and if they don't confess right now, they gotta leave. She *dramatic* like that. She always end up taking 'em back tho. She real big on not lying and even bigger on forgiveness. L.A. real big on a lot of stuff, but not that good at handling what it means to see folk for who they is. That's always hard for her. She always talking about how people can change.

TREE HOUSE

MS. BIRTH GOT TIME FOR most things except running back and forth in her house letting out all the good air. I love it cause she always got new food cooking even though the kitchen mostly smell like hot comb and week-old stovetop grease. She the first person to feed me pig's feet out of a jar. Say the secret is in the hot sauce and even though it's good denna mug, I ain't ate none since. I can't grasp the texture. It's my favorite house on the block because all my friends—her grandkids—are there. They stay directly across the street from us so we don't call my presence a playdate. It's just called *Can you watch Kendra tomorrow for me after school?* And she never say no cause it really ain't no difference between watching four kids and watching five.

All her grandkids older than me but we go to the same school, San Jacinto Elementary. They in real grades. I ain't in no grade at all. I'm in pre-K. But nobody act like it; especially Juice—who still too young to have to feel so obligated to be anything even though she the oldest grandchild and our guide. She take us on all our candy-stealing store missions, show us how to cuss, antagonize the rottweiler in my backyard, and is the reason we end up at Juan's. She hear about the tree house and makes him let me, her, and her cousin in through the backyard gate to see if he lying.

He ain't. It's a ladder hanging off the side of the pecan tree trunk and everything. & we climb up.

Before we even sit down good, Juan already know we impressed by his kid house; basking in the awe he predicted on our faces. It's all decked out with blankets and snacks all over the place. It's a whole new world. But before we even get the chance to get comfortable in it, Juan—who ain't as young as me, but ain't as old as Juice—asks nobody in particular if we ready for a surprise.

"Yeah," "No," and "What?" me, Juice, and her cousin say in unison. At this point I think the only better thing he could possibly present is a secret chamber that got a TV with cable on it, but we all look up at him from the floor and wait on the surprise.

In one swift—obviously overly rehearsed motion—Juan pulls down his pants and puts his penis in our face. The thing is barely outside of his body at this point and look a lot like spam. Bologna even; which I hate, even when it's burnt with crispy edges and mustard, but I immediately understand why kids be calling them weenies because his look exactly like a mini Oscar Mayer. Like the weenies they feed you at baby showers. & when Juan holds his in his hand, it looks like one thing. Camouflaged—like if he ain't have fingernails, his palm and penis would unite under holy matrimony and never let each other go. Like it's his most prized possession even at eight. Or seven. Or ten. Even in its infant, flaccid state—he knows how it can scar a room; & he's proud of himself.

Once we get over the initial shock of the sight, we begin playing our positions of various stages of disgust:

Me: afraid of catching cooties

Juice's cousin: throwing the snacks I desperately wanted to eat at his head

and Juice: sternly advising him to put his lil-ass dick away before she beat his ass in his own backyard. We all hop up to rush back down the ladder as quickly as we climbed it as Juan hangs his head out of the tree-house door. Staring us all down. Showing off his baby teeth. He laughs as we take off running toward the gate, still holding on to the place where pee gotta sprinkle out from. He laughing, not thinking nothing he did is technically wrong. But we all know what wrong is, and we all know not to talk about wrong things to no adult no matter how much they assure us they the open books they parents weren't for them. We know parents who say they open to secrets never know how to handle them once children start spilling. They start questioning your secrets for being secretive; so agreeing to hush ain't even a conversation we need to have amongst ourselves. We know when they ask *What ya'll was doing over there?* to respond with *Nothin. Building*

a tree house. We automatically know how to say *Nothin* so it don't seem like we asked for it. Plus, we don't really wanna get Juan in trouble even if we know Juan ain't gone get in trouble. He our friend; so we keep the image within our girl group, laugh about it to ourselves once we make it out his backyard and onto Ms. Birth's porch safely.

When we see him the next day tho, we don't talk—we just start swinging, hitting him upside the head with our barely balled-up fists as he cracks up, bent over from taking cover, while promising to pull it out again.

EXPIRATION DATE

MR. ALIGNMENT TELL L.A.: "**YOU** know yo husband been riding round to and from work every day with ol' girl, dontcha."

He say it real casual, like a friend asking if you wanna go get something to eat, cause that's the way he observes. Mr. Alignment know every single thing that's going on at the V.A. at all times like he getting paid overtime to do so, but he also L.A.'s oldest work friend—literally and figuratively, working there longer than she been alive. Actually, he been alive longer than anybody been alive, kinda like Morgan Freeman. They remind me of each other in more ways than one. All height and general old-man lankiness. Both built like bottle rockets. But he always look out for L.A. And he know we got this ash-black pickup that don't leave our driveway because L.A. and Doll share a 1994 burgundy-reddish Taurus to get to work where she make nutrition plans for patients while simultaneously putting literal pounds of brown sugar in her yams at home; & Doll work in the kitchen, cooking the meals and preparing the trays for those admitted patients. L.A. got a lot of friends in general, but men folk especially flock to her, filing in way back from her childhood. They can never understand what the word friend mean tho, so they keep waiting around to be her man. I swear it's clear as day, but I'm not allowed to say the word swear cause L.A. say that's not a good thing to say, but all the mens be low-key in love with her. & Mr. Alignment say one and two ain't adding up cause he see Doll in the car all the time with a woman, but the woman ain't her.

Maybe Doll sense this and that's why he starts accusing her of being sneaky first even though he be upping and leaving in the Taurus without telling nobody when he'll be back. Telling L.A. how she ain't gone be able to use the car this or that day and that he can just "drop us off."

Men are jealous. She say all the time. It's one of my first lessons on life.

They be jealous of you

yo family,

yo fun,

yo talents.

From the very beginning too.

Pay attention.

Don't ever be with no jealous man.

BUT DOLL AIN'T JEALOUS OF Mr. Alignment cause L.A. make it known to anybody who'll listen that she will never in life be attracted to no old man and finds it creepy for them to be attracted to her; so it's ironic how the old man is the one to get him caught up.

"What girl?" L.A. asks. When she give me the *men are jealous* speech, she forgot to tell me about the *men are messy* one cause Mr. Alignment don't waste no time giving her the first and last name of said girl, knowing all she finna do is find her. And quick.

"I don't know if you aware of this," L.A. prefaces once she gets the woman on the line, "but don't get in my car no more. I know you know he married."

Naturally, the next step is for L.A. to shape-shift into a spy. Since Doll don't really care about being married, and niggas in general lack respect for they wives; he still dip out in the car and leave us stranded. She goes and gets an extra set of keys to the Taurus made—hop on the bus way before Doll's shift is over—finds her car in the V.A. parking lot—opens up her car door—gets in said car—and waits

until Doll exits the building

with a group of coworkers, and ol' girl, yet again.

When L.A. sees them approaching, she leans the lever of the driver's seat back as far as it can go so they won't see her until she wants to be seen. When Doll reaches for the door handle— L.A. ejects the seat back to its original slope like a cat light on its feet—smashes her foot against the gas pedal—pulls off on they ass—and die laughing the whole way back to Prichard Lane; proud of herself for getting away with confiscating her own car. Speeding to San Jacinto Elementary to get me.

I'M SITTING ON THE FLOOR in a circle with my classmates when L.A. skips over them, picks me up, and races us back out the door like she in ninja training. It's like she knew as soon as we got back in the car, Doll would pull up. Which he does—in the ash-black truck I thought didn't work—so I don't got time to get buckled in cause he tries blocking us in the parking lot. It don't work, cause L.A. drive like she in a NASCAR race on a day-to-day basis so it ain't hard for her to veer the Taurus back out onto the road. Which makes Doll start to race us; chase us, I mean, since he real good at driving too. Something about it all makes my heart beat real fast even though my face is emotionless, but it feels as if the street clears out for us; not one other car on it, and the more L.A. speeds—the closer Doll maneuvers his truck into our lane as if his goal is to remove us from it completely. Every time he catches up, the closer he gets to our doors where I'm sitting in the back seat. If he decides to deviate the wheel and follow through with the swipe—it's me who'll get hurt.

Doll screams out of his window, casually—one hand on the steering wheel and the other hanging out the window like he finna ask a driver to let him over, except he's demanding L.A. to "PULL THIS SHIT OVER!!!"

The both of them fight to see who can get louder than my heartbeat, because all L.A. do is lean across and scream back "YOU SEE THESE KIDS IN HERE!!!"

I'm not doing nothing in particular besides looking out the window at Doll and wondering what all this is for when it's all as simple as him saying he got a girlfriend so he can get free and her breaking up with him so she can be too. None of this that's happening makes sense to me, but Doll looking kinda open. The wind blowing his face back, turning him red as his eyes. He ain't looked at me once, but I hope maybe I'm on his mind because he slows the truck down. It's not about us getting away more than he letting us go. Maybe he realize he don't really care, just needed to get the upper hand. Maybe he realize we gotta come home eventually, even if we gotta wait out everybody's adrenaline.

"PUT SOME SUGAR IN HIS tank," L.A.'s aunt advises once we get over there and she learns why. The suggestion seem too extreme. Too risky. So L.A. don't fill the tank with sugar, just sprinkle a lil bit in as a reminder to her root issue: *Nigga, you gone tell me I can't drive my car with my daughter while you riding around another woman!* Then the truck stop working forreal this time.

I think.

It's all too much. All too stupid.

I don't ever wanna be in love.

DRAIN

BEFORE PRICHARD LANE, I THOUGHT I made my first-ever friend named Drain in Trinity Place—the apartments right up the street. Then Drain ran over the bottom half of my body with her bike.

I don't see her cut the corner cause we in the circle of the court-yard and cause it's the first time somebody who ain't one of my cousins knock me down on purpose even when I'm already bending so voluntarily close to the concrete. Probably down making mud pies under the stairway, slapping and shaping shit on top of soil and calling it a delicacy. Probably playing follow-the-leader with all the older kids; you know how they like to make you do they dirty work. & I'm left-handed and clumsy. I don't know what it amounts to, but people stay pointing it out every time something I do turn out messy—like going outside and coming back bloody. I'm about three. Or thirty. I don't know what I'm doing on the ground, but I grow to love it. I'll sit on the carpet before a couch, lay across a rug before a bed. It's not about feeling closer to the earth. It's about stability.

Everybody start assuming the moon on my skin is a birth-mark, a waxing crescent cater-cornered on the left side of my left thigh due to the way it's misplaced, the way it look infinite. Like maybe that's the reason L.A. gave me it as a middle name and wasn't tryna be funny at all. Like she really thought I'd last forever. Like my first permanent scar ain't a scar but a birthright, a blood oath.

WE LIVE ON THE FIRST floor of the main building and Drain live in the building across from us and got a Mexican mama. Doll look more like Drain's daddy than mine. But me and her ain't the same. Or siblings. We all know it. Even the kids. Drain is older,
prettier
softer, and somehow more
innocent because of it. More believable because of it, which is probably why when she hunts me down, I'm asked to give a reason as to why she mighta did it. But all I can think about is how much I love her name. How you don't know if she is a she unless you know her personally, cause only girls will tell you to yo face how they meant to hurt you.

If she was less calculated, she coulda been a he or a nothing and maybe that's the reason I'm so drawn to her distance, her age, her height. Her legs; their length. All these elements mixing her up into something beyond reality. I don't wanna be her, I just wanna be believed then left alone. I can't explain it, what I would give to be nameless like that, bodyless like that; to be heard without having to explain

that Drain the one who taught me how to sniff out the soft spots to dig off into in the first place. Which areas give you the best chance at not descending. I guess I started doing it too well, too easily—pushing out pies like I'm getting paid for it, and now she mad, pumping her pedals around the courtyard on a mission. First lapping the corner and then my legs and laughing. Now I'm on the ground for real cause it's my safest home once the blood start pouring out my body like a profession. I can't believe how rubber is the thing that got me out here seeping.

Doll supposed to be watching us—or at least me—but he out there in the parking lot with his head under the hood working on the car with the music up too loud to see. It take me not getting back up—for all the commotion of childhood to stop—for anyone to notice how long I been down. Sometimes it feel as if I was born tryna prove pain don't faze me, but I'm holding on to my thigh with both hands like if I let go—it'll fall right off my hip same way Doll's ribs be falling off the bone. I swear they always on my mind.

The sight of blood makes me feel disillusioned and only starts to hurt because I thought Drain liked me. I even told L.A. she was my best friend. I always been an extremist like that. Either something is the best thing to ever happen or it don't matter at all. Either I'm immediately in love or I never will be. Either the answer is yes or the answer is no. Either I know or I don't. Either I feel one thing forever or I feel nothing at all. It's how I learn to hold on to it all. Gray be feeling ungodly.

MY INSIDES GUSH OUT AND I only start to scream because I think that's what I'm supposed to do. Doll carry me and L.A. meet us at the door like I barely survived a drive-by; my whole knee now wet and drippy with sticky stuff I can explain but Doll keep describing Drain's directness as an accident.

I don't get how two people who work at a hospital both immediately misdiagnose the problem: what bile be bringing out of people. How they both start acting like the police; L.A. the interrogator and Doll the donut eater and both of them putting the weight on me to do they job for them.

L.A probably volunteered to clean me up cause she volunteer to do all the work for everybody and maybe that's why she enjoys being on her back. It's one of the only times work gets to leave her. Any other time she gotta take up space. She gotta plug all of our bloody entrances. She got a lot of jobs; holds a lot of names; her main one she get from her job—a last name that's hers and one last name that's mine. Sometimes when I call her Mama, she don't even be answering until I call out her government. Like she dissociating from the role. We both do. It's how I get just as many nicknames.

> Kendra
>
> Kia
>
> Kool-Aid
>
> Crazy
>
> Ken-Ken
>
> Sneaky
>
> Brainwashed
>
> Bookie
>
> True Blood

And I answer to all of 'em. I love being called on.

Some folk even be calling me by my middle name—Infinite. Doll get this one tattooed on his bicep—but he gets it spelled the right way, which is not my way. & I see it finally, how it ends with me asking Y. Every single time. And I spend too many hours laying on my back on the floor thinking about what it means to have my name and face on a man's body and still not be recognizable. And I spend too many hours laying on my back on the floor wondering why L.A. gets my initials tattooed over her titties in a spot that fades the easiest. And I wonder why they both bled for me; because even when this blood gets wiped out of my thigh, it bubbles back up. We ripple it and call it love

it's how it becomes our representative.

EVERYTHING'S FOR SALE

DOLL MOVE IN WITH HIS brother while L.A. have a garage sale in our front yard but don't sell nothing. She gives it all away.

"That was one of the funniest thangs I eva SEEN!" Ms. Birth say as she walk us out to tell L.A. what she saw going on at our house before it happens. I look at her bend over at the waist tryna hold in her cackling. "That man tried to go through the front door . . . key wouldn't work! He tried it a whole lotta times too, looking at the key like it was crazy." She cracking up, forgetting to breathe her breaths real good and it make me laugh too even though I ain't really sure what's funny.

"Then he went around to the back . . ." she pause again for some more dramatic, comedic effect. ". . . key ain't work . . . AGAIN!" By now Ms. Birth hysterical, slapping her knees real good like she catching mosquitos. "He had his friend wit him too, girl. His friend was just shaking his head back and forth. He couldn't believe it. Doll was standing there wondering a long time why the key wasn't working, chile. He ain't know what the hell was going on."

"Cause I changed the locks," L.A. confess. & I turn my head her way. "He ain't gone be running in and out the house taking and hiding keys and breaking stuff." It seem like stuff being compromised is the only thing that make L.A. move.

SOMETIMES I GO VISIT AND Doll teach me how to play checkers in his room. I get real good when I play with the red checkers and even learn how to beat him. He tells me I can come see him anytime I want. Then he get somebody to put a down payment on this Cadillac that's the color of your tongue after you suck on a green apple Now & Later for too long that he adores and he get too busy to play checkers. He love his car so much that whenever I'm in it, he hands me a rag and makes me wipe down his windows if I lean on them.

Then something happens and L.A. let him move back in; trades in the Taurus for a boo-boo-green Ford Explorer so it's easier to carry everybody. But that's the only thing that changes.

Doll end up leaving again. It's his choice this time. He move back to his hometown of Houston for good and me and L.A. gotta leave Prichard Lane after the landlord gives Doll back the deposit and ups the rent. I don't see Ms. Birth or none of my friends no more until somebody die years later.

L.A. turn thirty-three and we spend a lot of time in the Explorer listening to "Hey Ladies" by Destiny's Child on repeat even though she won't divorce Doll until seven more years, but come home bald-headed once me and her move into a one-bedroom.

Then L.A. start driving us back and forth to Houston to see Doll and pretend it's all for my sake until Doll don't answer none of her calls when we get there once because he with his other girlfriend. Then we wait.

Then L.A. listen to "You and Me" by Musiq Soulchild the three hours back when she think I fell asleep; but I'm listening—with her—as she cry with all the windows down. I watch the sun set behind us through the side-view mirror and understand why it's her favorite time of day.

Then it becomes my favorite time of day. Then L.A. never

spend another half a day driving us back to Houston after she come home bald-headed again for the last time. I grow up, and help L.A. raise me by growing up and entering into some typa sister-wives union. We wed, and we move through time and travel together while singing the entirety of Mary J. Blige's *Mary* as we pack almost yearly. She start taking us to Uncle Needy's church every other day for sixteen years straight.

PART I

BLOOD

NEVERLAND

I START TO EXPLAIN HOW everything feels fake to a certain extent. How everything feels the same. Is—the same. Every emotion oddly similar. Except for the anger. That the anger is the only part of myself that feels real and sustainable. The only part of myself that's lasted because I've settled for it. How sometimes I wanna be really, really violent and how my flaw of being too nice only makes me wanna be even more violent when he asks me "So, why are you here?"

I don't really feel like—don't necessarily know how to explain it any further. I hope he just gets it. I mean, getting it is kinda his job.

"Sometimes I don't know the difference between what was dreamed and what really happened. Or if what really happened and dreaming . . . imagining . . . is the same thing, is . . . accurate." I say.

"I'm not sure what you mean." He asks, "Like what?"

Even though I'm here on my own accord—I feel like I'm testing him, baiting him. Like I came here as an experiment and not for help & maybe this is the actual problem I need to be working through.

"Just childhood stuff."

"What was your childhood like?" I can see him trying hard to be the opposite kind of person I've been complaining about since we met. & because this is about profession (or psychology), I'm the perfect patient for him to put his training to the test seeing as how I'm depressed enough to overexplain everything.

"It was the best. I'm an only child but it was always a lot of kids around." I follow up the statement with easily remembered monumental moments like seven-year separations and secrets and lies and skin and sex, but that's stuff any child with or without kinfolk experience at some point. "I had a lot of fun as a kid though. I got to figure out what I'm good at."

I complicate it when I get no reaction. I know part of his job is about being obtuse to a certain extent in order to make me feel as if I'm making big strides on my own.

"I got to be a person, I got to try out a lot of things, got to meet a lot of people. Even though it's kinda scary to be a daughter. A specific thing to be a daughter." I add on. "Especially now since it's a lot of lil girls in my family. I be scared for them. For they voices. But I had more fun times than not for sure." I remember aloud. I tell him how I don't think I ever want a daughter—who is the only daughter—or the first daughter—or the last. How all of those things are very particular positions to play. How maybe I don't want kids at all.

"What's scary about being any of those daughters?"

"Whatchu mean?" I start fidgeting with my fingernails. The answer is everything. They long now, but I don't bite them no more. One day I got on a plane and stopped.

"What do you fear?"

"You know, just people touching them, hurting them, silencing them. Stuff like that."

He writes things down again.

"And has any of those things happened to you?"

"I don't know." I say it so quickly I believe in it. So much of what he asks me is answered with "I don't know."

He don't say nothing back. I don't like silence, I just like being alone.

"I don't know." I say again. "Yeah. Prolly." I properly answer, referring back to my constant confusion of what is dreamed and what has happened. "I think so."

"Why are you unsure?"

"Cause . . ." I start the sentence with part of a word, "I was sleep when what I think happened, happened. I coulda been dreaming. That's why. My dreams be weird like that sometimes . . . repetitive." I repeat.

NINE

THE YEAR I TURN NINE, L.A. tells me how it happened. This *it* being the unspoken thing—this possibility—that looms over us until we die. She sits me down on the brand-new couch she picked out for our new house; the cushion uncomfortable. Foreign. My back now accustomed to the solid state of lowliness. I don't really see no noticeable indication of concern plaguing her face before, after, or as she tells me about the time someone had sex with her. She sits in one of the dining room chairs from her brand-new kitchen with the hardwood floors she's always wanted and asks me do I know what rape is in the same tone she asked if I knew what sex was when I was six. She says she was nine years old. How it got dark. How she was hanging with her sister who was hanging with her even older friends in an empty apartment. That when it was time to go home, she didn't know where she was to get back there. How her sister told her to wait before leaving her in a room with two teenage boys. Two cousins. That they kept staring at her and whispering. That she knocked on the door her sister was in to tell her to hurry up because the boys kept tryna touch her. That her sister told her to stop acting like a baby and sit down before she come out and beat her up. That the two boys grabbed her and put her in a nameless closet, held her down, took off her clothes, and took turns breaking the levee of her child body. That there was blood the way she always told me there would be blood. How the blood mixed with water. How she had just started her period for the first time days before. How she couldn't fight too long.

How this   is [the infant state]
How this   is [closed lips]

How her body was overpowered by almost man. Our generational overpowering of almost man. How all any of us can do is wait until it's over. How she sat balled up in the closet until morning, until her sister came back for her. How there was no sound, no audible future, as she attempted to wrap her body back around her body. How the sound only revealed itself again once she was found. How she was scolded for acting all weird in front of her sister's friends by hiding in closets. How nobody noticed the way something had gone terribly wrong. How maybe they noticed, but don't know how to say they wish they had a more practical place to hide once too. How L.A. only ever tells Doll and a therapist, who encourages her to tell me. How I'm nine. How L.A. gets terrified for me this year; fearing for my whereabouts and making sure to ask me about my body and who is touching it or had it already been touched. How she never talks to me about touching other bodies because no blood is involved in touching other bodies and blood is our only proof. How we never word it this way. How I start to think maybe sex is the scariest thing in the world. How I ask her how to know if someone has been raped. How she tells me about a test you get at a hospital instead of *because they say they were*. How the test is really invasive. How things get digged off into your canal. How this type of penetration is not sex at all. How this test won't even matter—won't even count—if you take a shower. How I wonder who wouldn't wanna take a shower, who wouldn't wanna burn off all their cells and walk around with no holes. How I think it's torturous how we're made with so many entrances. How wholeness has always been unattainable. How when L.A. exits that closet, she leaves out accelerated. How she has to see those boys all the time after. How they sit on the block. How they're friends with her friends. How they speak to her sometimes as she walks home from school or to the corner store for bread. How they smile at her. How they wave. How she's too young to fully comprehend what torment is but young enough to know fear. How she's always scared, but still speaks back. How she lives an okay life. How the days don't die. How come to find out, she had only been around the corner from her house the entire time.

NINE

THE YEAR I TURN NINE, I tell no one how it happened. This *it* being the unclear thing—this dream state—that looms over me right before I think about dying. I fall asleep in a bed I'm familiar with; the mattress picked apart. Similar. My back pressed up against it. I tell him how I don't really see nothing before or after I wake up with a penis inside of my palm. He asks do I know what molestation is in the same tone he asked me how my day has been six minutes ago. I say I think I was nine, but probably seven. It got darker. How I been dark before that, but family is important. That it was a Saturday morning and I spent the night at my uncle's house because L.A. went on a cruise or sum. That I ain't old enough for adults to think anything is off about kids sharing beds. How if I'm seven or eight or nine, Never is thirteen or fourteen or fifteen; but I backpedal

make us younger to make it sound improved. Never's my cousin. That I block it out because he's a kid too right? That my dreams be weird like that sometimes. That I was sleep. That the motion of my wrist stirred me awake; like a wave; like an ocean. That it moved in and out of the circle he made of my lifeless hand. That it was like a thing unattached to a person the way it fit. That being *scared* to move as a visual description is irrelevant although I was scared to move. That

I couldn't move, too scared to turn around and see him looking back at me. That I wouldn't know what to do if he was.

    How this is [the infant state]

    How this is [closed lips]

 How I had to force myself to open my eyes. How my right hand
moved up and down under the covers. How maybe back and forth
is the correct way since I was laying on my left side. How it swallowed my hand. How it felt like something I shouldn't be holding.
Something I haven't held in my hand since. How it felt like rubber with ripples, until it didn't. How it became

 like pressure that refused to bend. Steel in my tiny knuckles.
How I finish the story in full, say it aloud for the first and only
time. That within one of these states, someone I love(d) grabbed
my hand under the covers and made it touch their penis until I
stroked myself into consciousness, until I petted myself into a
paralyzed state. How I stared at the same spot on the windowsill
for what felt like way too many minutes until I was able to slow
my heart rate enough to stretch my legs out. Slowly. From knee to
chest to toe to edge, hoping this would let him know I'm awake/
would make him stop. How when I do, it's like the tide immediately recedes. How quickly he removes his penis from the hole he
made of my hand. & I hear it drop to the sheets like a pen.

DISCHARGE

SOMETHING'S WET. HANGING; STRUGGLING
to fall outta my body and into the water. I
feel it, and open my legs like I'm finna ash a cigarette. It seems
endless; the abyss of a drain; like it could swallow children,
shrink them; blow them back to birth; start them over. I snatch
off a piece of tissue that's thin enough to be an acid tab and don't
technically wipe, but tap it against myself; pulling it back to my
eye area to access, flipping it through my fingers like a baton.
I can't see things clearly anymore so I squint hard. The tab is
damp, but it ain't pee. I grab more tissue, pad way too much of it
around my palm and wipe for real this time—front to back the
way L.A. taught me after doing it the opposite way for so long.
Forward has always felt . . . right. But whenever I got caught
wiping that way, she'd lecture me about how wiping forward
would only bring the dirt out of me. Or—most accurately—leave
it in me.

"MAAAMAAAAA" I call out for her the moment my blood
begins to flow. I can hear the wind as she turns the corner of our
one-bedroom's one bathroom, scaling it in four steps.

"What?" she say as she walks in with too much attitude for
me. I wanna tell her *don't "what" me* like she always telling me,
but it's still too early. I ain't nobody's morning nothing. I'm still

half asleep on this toilet, leaning over my knees with my face in my empty hand when it shoulda already been washed by now.

"Get up, Kendra. And brush yo teeth, we gotta go." I show her the piece of tissue, extend my elbow toward her face to expose the sliver of red lining wobbling like a slinky across the starch whiteness.

"I started," I state. She bend down, start digging in all the stuff under the sink; the razors, the cotton balls, the Q-tips, the tub of Vaseline, the lotions that smell good yet do nuthin bout abolishing ashiness, and once she stands back up—she hands me a pad.

"I started at nine so I was waiting," she say, and places a stack of them on top of the sink. She bleeds a whole lot, still. But hers is different. It can last months at a time and although I don't like how she says she started instead of why it keep lasting so long, I'm too busy thinking bout how I'm gone maneuver the rest of the fourth grade now that I'm a woman to correct her statement. Once I get to school, I convene all my fourth-grade friends in the restroom, make them gather in a circle around the stall so I can give them the same lesson L.A. gave me since I'm the first of us to start.

"Told ya'll I was bleeding." I get different variations of *Do it hurt? How it feel?* And for a hater in the back, *Okay, and?* They peek in and I show them the barely wet pad through the side slits of the stall as I place the sticky part to the palm of my hand so the visual is clearer. I take the packaging from the fresh pad to roll up the used pad and seal it shut with the small sticky note that holds them together before rolling that up in tissue, using my knees to squat and steady myself before placing the fresh pad in the lining of my Powerpuff Girl panties.

"Don't put this in the toilet," I warn them. I don't know exactly what will happen if you do, but I just thought they should know.

"You need to change yo pad every couple of hours." L.A. reminds me. I'm barely bleeding; even though my tummy feels unsteady like I fell down the first drop of a roller coaster. But soon there'll be rivers of blood gliding down my thighs and sticking to my ankles and stapling my butt cheeks together as I knee-to-chest spring through the house because I overslept, or sneezed too hard, or coughed too rough, or simply existed. Sometimes there's so much blood I think I'm dying. I think I'm bleeding for my entire bloodline. It comes out like fruit punch, clear and to the point, thick in a way that lets you know the components of it are maybe not that good for you—like Hawaiian Punch. Sometimes it drops out of me in clots in showers, profuse like sickles. Sometimes I regret not having a penis. There ain't a panty I own without a stain or semblance of something that once happened making a guest appearance. There ain't a month where cleaning the blood shedding out of me don't feel like an omen. How the only thing I hope is to not turn my clothes into rags and the bathroom into the Red Sea once I pull down my panties.

Soon, it'll be days where I ruin school and sports uniforms and friends let me wear their jackets around my waist in order to hide my dried-up blood.

Soon, it'll be days where ibuprofen and things stop working.

Soon, it'll be days where I throw up while shitting blood and have to continue on with my day like nothing happened.

Soon, it'll be days where I cancel plans and curl up into empty tubs, unable to stretch a limb as sounds I can't describe project from my gut. & it's something that strips you; since you can't make it stop—the leaking.

"If yo teacher won't let you go to the bathroom," L.A. say, "just tell them what's going on. But you gotta change. Don't be leaving this same pad on all day, Kendra, that's nasty."

LOVE LANGUAGE

BY THE TIME I RETURN. L.A. already got a folding table picked out and wiped down and I start removing quarters outta my pockets by the dollar; making sure we got enough to clean and dry all our clothes. I take my job as the counter and securer of coins seriously, because if I don't—L.A. gone have us sitting in the Washingteria all hours of the night. I make sure to convince her that we need to go to the one off Ledbetter because it's bigger and got more appliances but really it got a jukebox so it's a favorite.

As soon as we walk in with our sacks of laundry, I make my rounds around the establishment until I find two empty baskets to confiscate, and roll 'em back to wherever L.A. at to throw our bags in.

"Alright," I say, and she hands me a twenty-dollar bill. Always.

I power walk to the back of the establishment where a money machine is installed on the wall where coins pop out fast like somebody hit the jackpot. It's right next a tampon machine; and sometimes boffum be out of order. When this happens; the owners will stand in a doorway and hand out coin wrappers by the fives. If you get there early enough—the machines do work; and the coins be loose so I gotta hurry to stuff them in every pocket of my school khakis until they start to sag a lil bit.

I make columns on the table—lay rows of 4x4 across it the same way my great-grandmother do whenever she give us money outta the flower vase she keeps all her change in.

"How many loads we got?" I ask as L.A. throws clothes into an empty washer that's way too small for its $1.50-per-load price point. I personally don't care bout separating clothes by color, but L.A. do—which is why this part is her job and the reason she ignores me when I say we could save more money—and more music—by throwing them all in there together.

"Uhhhh . . ." she look from the basket to the table to the washer, accessing the situation at hand. "Prolly bout five." I look up at her with the saddest of eyes. Do you know how hard it is to find five empty washers at the same time at a Washingteria on a Friday evening? We ain't never leaving. Then she say, "Well . . . seven, including the towels and blankets." I hate washing the towels and blankets. They always gotta get dried twice, which means the $1.50 a load is finna get doubled—so not only are we never gone get outta here—we might not even have that much change left over to listen to songs while we wait.

"Dang. Okay." I say under my breath—cause at this point, it is what it is—and start sliding the coins down the table toward her so she can start the cycles. "You got some more dollars?" I check just to be sure; I need to know, because I'm willing to not have clean clothes. I'm willing to give up a lot to be able to hear.

"*Go look in the car,*" I tell myself and walk closer to her hip, dig my hand into her pockets until I find the keys and run outside to ransack the car doors and car floors for change until I find enough silver to gift the jukebox. Because I got taste, I already know what I wanna hear once I return. I usually choose between a Brandy, Britney, or Beyoncé deep cut. Sometimes

Sisqó. Never none of the popular singles though. L.A. always choose somebody like Sade, Sting, or the S.O.S. Band—which is cool with me cause I love all them too so it's really like I picked the entire playlist.

THE FIRST TIME L.A. SAYS *Let me show you how to slow dance*, she whisks me up and down all the laundromat aisles like I'm Cinderella at the ball and "So into You" by Tamia plays in the background, so now we play it every time; turning our chore into something to look forward to. As the clothes enter cycle after cycle, we go back and forth, song for song, singing loud in these people's place of business, until we get to our last fifty cents for our last song—our song—that leads into our last dance—the finale—as our clothes enter their final dry cycle right before it's time to fold.

"The man hold you right here," she tells me—taking the lead, holding one hand at my waist while holding my hand too tight with her other so I won't struggle to keep up. "And you put yo hand right here."

I let her direct my body, move my right hand to her right shoulder, wondering why she opts out of them being wrapped around her neck like they do in all my favorite coming-of-age stories. I never slow danced with a man and I don't think it'd be underwhelming, but I'm worried about which position I'd wanna play; I know it can't feel like this. L.A. slides her hand across my lower back and I keep a close eye on my wrist instead of my feet. I trust my legs. I trust them to move and work and dance and run. I never know what my hands will do—will touch—without my permission even though this is now just our routine.

We do this—we ~~sway~~—with or without the music as other clothes washers watch on—move out of our way—or stand in it as we slide down their lanes.

Sometimes they smile.

Sometimes they look annoyed. But they never interfere. I don't even think we'd notice if they did.

AFTER SCHOOL SPECIAL

—But I'm always thinking of Reign

—The way she wear her hair

—Straight back in a ponytail

—How I'm so far away from where she is

—Waiting after school to see her

—How I'm always at the rec

—Sometimes long after everybody gone

—How on these days I help myself

—& adults trust me

—with too much, so I manage things I ain't got no
   business managing
—I pull the mats out the back of the bleachers and let her
   in through the back door
—We lay on the blue ones while she show me stuff on her
   phone
—Doll say he gone get me a phone soon
—Reign don't like going home, cause she gotta answer too
   many questions
—Her house right down the street
—If she take too long, her grandma gone figure out where
   she been
—She always worried
—Reign getting tied up wit boys but Reign be talking
   to me

—bout all the boys her grandma don't want her getting
   tied up with
—The other girls her age don't like that
—They think if boys like Reign, then boys can't and/or
   don't like them
—I don't understand why it matters what they like
—when they only like whatever it is they think other
   boys like
—& Reign know this too,
—Reign tell me she don't like none of them
—But she like that they like her, which is really all I think
   I want too
—but this don't stop them from laughing

—every time she walk by. I hate how being a girl means
—you automatically get thrown into hierarchies
—It's so much room on the mats
—I don't like how everybody stay comparing
—Reign
—the most quiet, nicest, softest girl I know
—So bad I wanna run over to the other girls and say they
  betta start being nicer to her
—Quiet or not, we all still end up a similar type of empty
—I think she so pretty,

—because she always alone

—Which makes her calm in my mind

—It ain't got nothing to do with how she look, but how she
hold her head

—I slip up and think she a woman

—I'm too busy falling in love

—with Reign too

—I take whatever she say to heart

—I don't know another way to tell Reign I admire her

—Because the way she show no fear

—make me wonder what happened to her

—Reign say it don't matter what people know, it's about
what they think

—and all they minds been made up when it comes to her

—I don't mind making up the rest of the semantics since

—Reign don't lie about how lonely making your own
decisions can be

—That whatever we don't tell one another is the exact
reason I like her so much

—This thought feels better than admitting it's a
possibility that it matters

—if I claim to care about her

—When Reign lays next to me, she says stay

—young as long as I can

—That rushing don't do nothing but make you sad too
  early

—Really I just wear braids and try hard

—to be happy

—since I'm already sad

—At home I practice in the bathroom mirror what I'd be
  like at Reign's age

—even though my ponytail ain't got no hang time

—I have full two-sided conversations with myself

—In my perpetual yearning for the future, I create

—scenarios of what I would say to boys especially once
  I'm big like her
—I wonder would I call them *baby* and let them touch me
  anywhere
—Nah,
—I wonder would I call them *baby* and whether they'd let
  me touch them everywhere
—Is it all in a look? Am I sexy
—if I raise my eyebrow this way and lean my chin down
  slow? Do I care?
—How do I make 'em never get over me even if I'm over
  them?
—Would they still call even if I stop answering? Do I care?
—Reign say it don't take all this extra

—effort. It don't take no effort at all

—Reign is right

—But I still think of what she would do if somebody not
me laid down next to her

—What she'd do when he asked her *What's wrong? Are
you okay?*

—Would she answer with the truth?

—Would she correct them?

—Would she go along for the ride?

—Would she lie with them?

—Would she be able to fall asleep?

Return to sender.

Return to sender.

Return to sender.

Return to sender.

Return to sender.

Return to sender.

Return to sender.

Return to sender.

Return to sender.

DISMOUNT

LET'S JUST SAY I'M RETURNING from something

    when I turn in bed in the middle of the night. I'm six. Nine. Seven

            is a lucky number, I've been told. A symbol of completion. & ending cycles is cool I guess, but don't nobody ever talk about how it means the very next day—a new one gotta begin. Again. I'm a wild sleeper. A sheet kicker. So at some point, I usually feel L.A.'s body connecting to my wrist or foot, but I don't. All I hear is breathing by my back and a slight knocking against the wall. It keeps speeding up and slowing down; the sound rocking my eyelids until I'm alert. It's a reoccurring scene of life.

    I turn; do the same slow blink that happens whenever I'm tryna stay awake in Doll's truck in the middle of the night. He a truck driver now. First as a milkman and now as his own man. & sometimes he be letting me pretend to drive it. I sit on his lap and maneuver the wheel slowly with both hands while his foot controls the gas. I learn all the truck's functions and how to swerve in and out of lanes. If I tag along, it don't matter what time his shift starts—I make myself awake. I don't wanna miss out on seeing the world. I don't need nobody remembering my memories for me. When I turn in bed, I rub my eyes real good until they squeak. I don't know what I expect to see, but seeing Doll in our bed when I haven't seen him for months ain't it.

He says, "Hey."

I say, "Hey," back.

& turn back around, face a wall this time. Not in a shocked and fast way, but in a steady roll one does when they typically don't expect to see their married parents who live in two different cities and in two different residences having sex in the middle of a school night in the bed the child shares with their single mother.

That type of turn.

I'M ALWAYS IMAGINING HOW SEX will be, so I'm not scared, I don't think. Mostly I'm kinda annoyed at how it's their home, or a bridge, or a marriage made weak and mindless so maybe sex is a haven or an anchor or the downfall; but I'm not disgusted, just hazy.

L.A.'s legs are on top of Doll's shoulders so when he greets me with "Hey"—he's leaning forward between them. His elbows are locked on each side of her and their navels are almost touching even though he ain't that close to her face. They're both naked, and seeing L.A. with no clothes on ain't distracting at all because we always naked around here; but Doll's shoulders and chest hair and back and butt is. Despite seeing penises, I've never seen this much of a man in person before and it feels mandatory.

They not under no covers in this dark room but Doll luminous. Yellow. His reflection outlined on the wall behind him. It's all how I imagined it to be, but not, since it seems safe and they both smiling. At least Doll is; and I'm not sure if it's because he sees me or because he's inside of his baby mama again, but I see this nigga's teeth clear as day and I regret my life.

When I turn their way, I don't sit up. I don't see nothing on him they would blur out on TV, just the halt of his bottom half slapping against L.A.'s bottom half and I catch myself wondering what it is he feels about exposure since I've never seen them stick together unless they're sticking together. Not holding hands or kissing or nothing like that—this, I never see; besides that one picture in the photo album where we're on the couch and I'm trying to pull their faces apart. By sticking, I mean laying on top of one another. I'm pretty sure it's the position whose image I was made in. It's prolly the only thing keeping them on speaking terms.

When they was actually together instead of married, Doll wrote L.A. love letters all the time. & because L.A. is a hoarder who keep every single piece of mail she's ever received, of course I find them over the years; on floors, inside trash bags and folders, and places like that. I find notes he wrote on shredded sheets of paper, professions on birthday and anniversary cards, and emails from when they was going back and forth to child support court. All his love letters are about how much he loves having sex with her. How he can't wait to come to Dallas and see her/touch her/enter her. How sex is the only thing I know about whatever love they could have possibly shared.

DOLL IS AN OCCASIONAL TYPE of man who gets to leave and I'm jealous; because he lingers; like the brown recluse venom that leaks outta my thigh that one year; leaves a hole in my body so wide, I don't even cry as doctors dig out the leaking pus with Q-tips they've dipped into antibiotics before entering them into me. I wonder if Doll does the same thing when he dips into L.A. If there's any precaution present. I bubble up in this energy since I gotta be the one to deal with the repercussions of all his lives. It's how I imagine it to be because it's hot, foggy. They both wet like they ran inside from a storm. It's not how I imagine because I realize the wetness is sweat. I see it drip off of Doll's forehead and onto L.A.'s face and it's gross but she don't seem to be complaining.

I wanna look down so bad, but this ain't just anybody's body. This is the body I was supposedly extracted from. & it feels dangerous; to learn that much about him. Looking down would taunt me, knowing whether or not I got my butt cheek hair from him or myself, or if I got the capacity to weather a child instead or the stamina to prioritize my own pleasure.

I force myself to focus on other factors like how a body get flexible, formidable even, when it's in conversation with another's. How L.A., who can't even touch her toes all the way without bending her knees all of a sudden got those same knees almost touching her ears. I wonder do she only believe in her body when it's being shaped. I wonder do she think her body is beautiful at all, because I never hear her say it. I wonder if she believes her body being so close to his means something, anything. I wonder if she think her body is worth care beyond this act that keeps getting mistaken for repair. How she stay preaching to me the importance of sex and the importance of waiting and the importance of having someone who honors your body and all its openings. Of having someone who loves you. & I trusted her word. Yet all that go out the front door every time she opens it in the middle of the night. How I don't think I like her when she's laying down or when we sleep in the same wound; because then I wonder if in it is how I got deceived.

If I'm ever mentioned at all in life or letter—I'm being offered up by L.A. as a side dish, but she never pushes the issue. And if Doll don't come over, nobody even tells me he's in town or seem to care that her baby daddy don't care to spend time with the baby more than he care about laying up in her body. She'll meet him at hotels—and I don't know how I always know when it happens, but I do. Everybody is always so obvious. Usually, L.A. start acting funny. I think this is what it means to be connected to someone—it's apparent when they start to drift away.

BEFORE THE DYING

WHEN WE GO AND GET my cousin Candy for the summer, her belly big like she just finished eating all the burgers in the bag and it hurt L.A. like it was me. I ain't sure if L.A. cry about it cause Candy only fourteen or because Candy ain't feel she could tell her she having sex, let alone pregnant; but L.A. pride herself on being helpful and close to all her nieces and nephews. At least she try to be—to the point where if I never have a baby, she been a grandma.

Either way, for five months, none of us know about it even though L.A. say she thought it was weird how whenever Candy was supposed to be watching me, she kept falling asleep. But besides this, nobody ever expected anything like this to happen since Candy is so responsible; doing what she supposed to be doing and being where she supposed to be.

ONCE HER BELLY OUTS HER. Candy always asking if I wanna touch my almost cousin inside her stomach, but I always say no and ask to watch *Space Jam* instead. It's the only movie I watch now since she stopped letting me watch *Friday* after I asked her "What's a big booty hoe?" in honest search of an answer. Sometimes she lifts her shirt to show me the limbs moving around in there anyway and it seems so fictional—like we in the end stages of a sci-fi film. I watch as her stomach shifts and contorts because an almost human done infiltrated her body. I don't get how the almost human don't sheer its teeth; don't deflate them both. I got a hard time understanding how a person can produce a brand-new person, how I see her whole life change, yet people still giving all the credit to a boy.

They keep telling me how we ribs, us girls. Not like the ones Doll be barbecuing, but the ones that can break and crush and renew over time. I don't condone the idea of being made. Created. Claimed. So I never repeat being a rib. It sound dumb. Especially since boys ain't gotta make the baby at all. Not all the way. They just help start the baby off when they let it out of their body before causing permanent damage to the girl's.

What I'm not so sure about is if you look under the boy's clothes or if he sees under yours; but I'm pretty sure Candy transferred my new cousin through laying down since that's how they do it on all the horror movies I'm too scared to watch. They always be out in the woods at night in a lone cabin for no reason at all and I always miss the killing but I be sneaking between my fingers to watch the kissing. They always start doing it with they mouths open and they eyes closed.

Then they lay down.

Then the boy gets on top of the girl.

Then the girl starts crying at some point.

Then one of them dies. It's always a penis involved before the dying. There's always a lot of rearranging before the birth, & Candy blooming like an Outback onion overnight only for her body to have to bust open reminds me how we always find out everything through the clothes; where it is we're softest.

THE FAST LANE

MY MAWMAW ASKS DOLL TO ask L.A. if I could come visit once, and L.A. tells him *She can come **every** summer.*

So I go every summer.

And sometimes Christmas. And L.A. cries for a week every-time I leave.

When I'm there, all my time is basically spent at my Banana's house—Doll's sister. I think she own the biggest house I ever been in cause she got a flight of stairs—which means opulence. An attic—which means extra space for extra stuff, and a washer and dryer in her kitchen, which means she rich and whenever I joke about it, her daughter Brie say slick shit like "I can't help that my mama did a good job raising me."

Like me—Brie is an only child, except she's accustomed to a lot more personal space than I am. I mean, she basically got her own apartment that we refer to as the second floor of Banana's house. The second floor is the center of all my Houston trips; the base where everything fun is planned out and executed, although every summer is significantly similar. & my annual presence interrupts that; since they make us spend every single day together from sunup to sundown solely based on us being close in age.

We spend weeks over our mawmaw's house running in and out of her kitchen all hours of the night. We ride down freeways listening to chopped & screwed music on the way to Galveston and swallow gallons of salty, dirty water while pouring cans of Pepsi into the salty, dirty waters of Galveston while trying not to die; tightening ourselves on the backs of adults as they survey into the deep end of what I still struggle to define as an ocean. We go to Astroworld, at least once, and I shout as somebody drags me onto all the rides I'm scared to get on cause Doll say he ain't pay for my ticket for nothing. Brie get ready to fight me because all my high energy be getting on her nerves. We go swim at anybody's available apartment complex pool and eat sandwiches and Capri Sun pouches out of a cooler, then wait thirty more minutes to get back in to avoid catching cramps, and at some point during the season, Doll barbecue while we sneak swallows of alcohol.

But whatever we do, we always end up back at Banana's at the end of most days. There, we prank call strangers that turn into real callbacks from strangers and police. We have up-all-nights that lead into all-day sleeping. Then me and Brie don't speak all school year, just to do it all again in nine months.

THE ONLY DIFFERENCE THIS SUMMER is that Banana got a new boyfriend who got way too many kids. Four boys, ranging from younger than me to early teen. & we do all our summer things—except this time, we do it with them.

They join me and Brie on the second floor where I sleep in her room, and they sleep everywhere else. I don't remember how their faces look, but I'm like ten—which means I'm not ten; but if I look hard and spend enough time with them, they all cute cause they a mystery, a reflection, & naturally, they start to make themselves believe they like the new girl around. & since it can't be Brie cause she almost they sister, it gotta be me, even if them being blood stands in the way.

It's one too many hits here and getting picked too often in games of Tag and Duck, Duck, Goose, that give me the impression I'm being pursued. Plus, after about two weeks there—all four of 'em straight up tell me they like me. Which I'm fond of. Not the liking me, but the directness. In fact, I kinda respect it. I don't like having to guess or assume things, even though it overwhelms me every time I exit Brie's room and one of them corners me.

"I'ma let you know later" is all I keep saying once the *I like yous* turn into *So which one of us you like?* This question get on my last nerve since I'm not sure why I'm expected to like any of them just because they made themselves like me. Especially since they all smell. Like all the time. How you musty in the mornings, I will never know. But it's a lot of odor in all the rooms. L.A. explains it to me: how we have to learn how to clean up blood as a part of our growth—having to force Lateral and Never and all my other boy cousins to consistently bathe themselves is a part of theirs. That she don't know what it is about water, but you gotta force boys into it; and even then you gotta watch, because they'll come out dry as a Texas summer. If you don't make them, they simply will not do it. And to know I'm supposed to make my summer boyfriend decision based on this intel—I gotta say—seems kinda tragic.

IN THESE BOYS' QUEST FOR me to choose, I begin to understand power: that I can pick

anyone I want. Not because I look so good or I'm the smartest person around or I'm just that damn irresistible—cause ten-year-old me is hit—but because the boys don't really got no control over they wants and the prospect of saying they won. That's clear. They want—need—me to choose one of them so they can prove to the other boys that they're the best boy. It's never really about me, it's about the potential they can flaunt their win of me in front of their brothers. It's about muscle, and I get that. But I don't like how whoever I pick will feel like a front-runner and, in turn, me—like a thing. So I take my sweet time with giving away what little I got. These ain't just boys I can spread my time between. I need to be sure in my choices before I commit. These are real-life brothers, and this alone means whatever decision I make will be irreversible, which means it can take me forever, which is why Brie decides the best way to get an answer to my dilemma is to pimp me out to her pre-stepbrothers.

REALITY DATING SHOWS ARE THE only thing going on and *NeXt* on MTV is a central part of our nightly three a.m. lineup. The show is the same every time, opening with five people riding in what seems to be a tour bus to what seems to be an empty parking lot to meet the person they're going on a date with. It's a gamble, literally, because you get paid one dollar for every minute you last—but mostly because one by one, as the people exit the bus, the person who's waiting outside of it can at any moment yell out "NEXXXXT!!!" which implies you ugly, a bad dresser, or both. Either way, they ain't finna continue the date. So back on the bus the rejected person goes.

As a watcher, you begin testing yourself to see how long you think you can last in either position, or to predict the moment where the primary dater can't take the antics of the other any longer. But all the show really be doing though is displaying how men be dense, women be desperate, and even the idea of attention is addictive; so all we can do as children with minimal resources is play into it by re-creating the scenario in hopes of leading me to true love; which is why Brie transforms her bedroom door into a busload of hoes.

Because Banana work nights and won't know how we got boys in the room with the door closed, Brie lines the brothers up outside her doorway from youngest to oldest as I get ready by hand ironing my pajamas. Even though my posture bad, I sit at the edge of her bed with my legs crossed at the knee so they think I'm classy. Sophisticated. Controlled. I figure if we role-playing, I gots to go all out.

Before the first one enters, I hear Brie ask them general questions like "What you want with my cousin?" and "If you had the money, where you gone take her? Where ya'll gone go?" I'm assuming this is the green screen confessional portion of the episode, but they answers drop me right back down into reality. The specifics don't matter cause they all align with nothing and nowhere and I have an epiphany as she lets the first one in that a man without a plan makes me nervous—and one without a speck of creativity or follow-through will never have nothing to do with me ever. But it's already too late. The show already started.

FIVE WORDS INTO THE FIRST date, I immediately know I ain't built for this. I know what I feel quick and plan accordingly, especially since I been chose the oldest one in my head from the jump. I don't see how they ain't figured this out yet—my need to escape my youth. I was just tryna wait until it was time to almost go back to Dallas, that way he could say he won, but I ain't have to see him no more to be reminded of it. But I care too much about the feelings of folk I don't even care about to "NEXXXXT" any of the boys on sight. I've spent enough time with them to learn their personalities, to know they nervous about being in rooms alone with me too; so I suffer along by finishing the game.

They file in and out like they on a conveyor belt. The only reason I send the youngest one back is because I feel like I can beat him up. The next one, I don't remember whatsoever. Not even a lil. Even when he leaves. The second to oldest one like *me* most; you can always tell in the beginning, which is why I never understand why we act so surprised when we settle and it turns out they don't. The ones who do be real tender with you, real aware of you. Not in a crush way where they stumbling over words and staring at you all bug-eyed. But in a way where they looking at you and seeing themselves. The eyes be easy. The point is, it's all kinda softly still about them. But Brie say he ugly and that she not finna let me pick him while I'm living under her roof even though I like *him* most too. I don't next him at all. We kick back. I uncross my knees. We chill. We joke. He leaves. I don't want him to.

I wish I was real enough to switch my decision last minute.

When the oldest brother sits down next to me on the bed, the first thing he asks is what his brothers said and/or did. I say "nuthin" cause it ain't none of his business, nor do I mention how much fun I had with the second oldest—who's still technically older than me, but just not old enough. This brother is fourteen; and I've spent my whole life wanting to be fourteen, and sixteen, and thirty-five, and forty.

"I like you" is all he says. All he been saying.

"I like you too" is all I say back because what else is there to say. It's the quickest date in the world. Straight to the point, the way I tell myself I prefer my life to be. He wins. I surrender. And I'm cool with him believing he's the deciding factor in the reason why.

When the mutual liking is confirmed, we both stand up from the edge of Brie's bed and hug. It's cute. Nicer than the normal kid hug with dinosaur arms. Nice in its unfamiliarity, seeing as how I deprive myself of this type of closeness without cringing. His body is larger, taller, and more trapped than mine, so the difference feels good. He seems cold, afraid, and don't know what to do with the moment besides planting his feet and breathing hard. I kinda want us to take off all our clothes, throw them in the dryer, and sway. It's more about the song I hear in my head than it is about him. Neither of us move tho. No backs are caressed. No booties are cuffed. No forearms are tightened. Then Brie bangs on the door and say we got three minutes. We sit in whatever this is supposed to be. We hold each other in the same spot, up by our backs, for 180 seconds. And the whole time I'm thinking how much I wouldn't mind holding his neck.

THEN BANANA HEAR ALL ABOUT our late-night date games cause boys are messy too
                    and talk
to they daddies. And the whole time I'm thinking how much I wouldn't mind holding on to somebody's neck when Banana comes stomping up the stairs one night. It's something she rarely do, but we being too loud while she tryna sleep again, so she comes to yell at us.

I don't really remember what else she says once a quick lil "witcho fast ass" gets chunked my way. But it's how I know she know.

Fast is a hereditary response. I'm sure Banana been called it before and now she paying it forward. But hearing it directed toward me in such a matter-of-fact way—like the path I'm headed down is glaring back at her—makes me wanna retreat, but also makes me wanna write. At school, I'm the last one "messing with them lil boys," but she say it so hard, I think it's true.

Really, *them lil boys* was being fast with me, but I don't say nun cause it don't matter and they ain't gone say nun cause they don't care. They quiet as a mouse when it's time to say what part they played, but can't shut the hell up any other time, telling folk what's going on and what they did and who they did it with and this why I can't fuck with them like that when they purposely use they power to play with me. I don't even try to guess which one told, I know whoever did told the story told it one-sided; mentioned me choosing but not how they mad they did or didn't get chose; but in my book they all waak forever for being so silent now.

Not one of them considers maybe I wanted more hugs, more dances to no music, more nights to say "I like you too," and figure out why. And now the opportunity to do so is extinct, because now I got a reputation; and because I don't get a choice in taking responsibility for what role I play in everything I do—I spend the rest of the summer acting like they dead. Cause they is. To me. We ain't hugging or hanging. I ain't smiling in nobody's faces. I don't kick it wit 'em, laugh wit 'em, nothing. Maybe this what Banana mean by *fast*. I move on fast. Talk too fast? Walk even faster? It's the first time somebody uses the word to describe me when I spent so much time distancing myself from behavior I thought defined it. It never works tho. It's not supposed to.

CHILD'S PLAY

PENCIL NUMBERING IS BASED ON a grading scale that relies solely on graphite's core hardness, which—under the right amount of pressure—has the capacity to convert into diamonds. I ain't never been into expensive jewelry, but I think the possibility is why teachers act like it's a crime to use anything other than a #2 pencil. It look better on paper and don't leave a cloudy shadow in case I need to erase parts of it, or all of it. I use the one with the long yellow body and thick tip to write my first letter about not being here.

The letter not once explicitly states I will—at some point—take myself out. I pick out my words as carefully as possible. The phrasing is more along the lines of *I wanna die*. The difference is always clear to me, but somehow indistinguishable to others whenever I try and explain how the letter is about wanting something to spite my face but not my hands. How I am simply wishing

myself away, turning a suicide letter into a *my inside feelings of worthlessness is at its heaviest right now and makes me wanna not be here to be perceived or praised any longer* letter. Me wanting to die since everybody will die won't cause as much ruckus, and I know that. Which is why I write that. I know misdirected blame only follows self-harm. I know there'll be no questioning, no research of why I feel worthless, more than there will be confusion about why I'm so ungrateful. I only know this because I almost die once when my baby cousin Lateral—Candy's son—tries to murder me the school year he lives with us. He spends every ounce of his free time watching wrestling practicing his Pedigrees on me, or watching *Child's Play* tryna see if all the things an evil doll gets away with is possible in real life.

Up until him being born, everybody picked on me on both sides of my family—chasing me around the house with Chucky dolls, jumping outta closets in gorilla costumes, and terrorizing my fear of everything simply because they could. So of course, I pay it forward the first five to seven years of his life.

I push him down.

I make him cry when I shouldn't.

I let dogs chase him. I tease. & this is why I assume he tries to snuff me out with a pillow. Lateral strong; way thick and solid now and can overpower most kids. It's how he catch me slipping, appearing in my bunk outta nowhere; but before I can realize what's happening to knock him back down—it's a pillow and a body over my face. I'm tryna swing, tryna kick, but it's moot because I know I'm ok.

My life is in danger of being snatched away, but this is the point; although I feel so bad, so guilty, for pushing Lateral to it. I feel so bad he'll think of me as a bad experience and not a good cousin. I feel so bad I let him beat me to it, that he'll get all the blame when this is what I been wishing for. So I'm screaming, but can't nobody hear it. Not even me, cause Lateral got the pillow sealed so tight under his weight that every time I try to open my mouth—the sound gets swallowed. Over and over, I try to breathe—even outta my ears—but it don't work, & I'm still alive. Only then do I reconsider the concept of losing my breath for good. Not because I fear the death—but because the dying take too fucking long.

. . .

I'm laying in the same bunk drinking out of a carton of strawberry milk Doll left in our refrigerator from one of his routes through our city with both of my feet up as I think about pillows and how I sleep under them now. Then I start writing my letter.

The way I'm jotting it all down, it look like my venting is homework. I'm an ideal student, can do school stuff in my sleep, so I never really need L.A.'s help. I don't struggle with completion—having a task makes me think I have purpose. It's the comprehension that gets tricky. I got the notebook sitting widelegged in the middle of a textbook and I'm working diligently because I fear forgetting ever having feelings and writing them down at a fast pace is the only way I'm aware they even happen; the only way I know how to make them stay. I don't know how to verbalize the things I feel about myself out loud without messing up and stumbling through it. Still don't. If I don't record it, it leaves me; so I hurry.

When I'm done, I stuff the letter into my backpack because I'm only eight. Maybe ten. Possibly eleven. Either way, I think I got more privacy than I do.

"KENDRA, WHAT'S THIS?" L.A. ASKS when she finds it the next damn day. The graphite barely smeared enough to lie, but I try to anyways when she holds it straight in my view. I squint my sockets real tight.

"Huh?"

"This letter, girl."

"Oh." I can't tell her about Brie's room this summer. She might say I was wrong too, so I say, "I was playing." Instead.

Something like that.

Nothing like that.

I don't really remember. I prolly try to make myself cry. Not from pain but embarrassment that I felt bad enough to write down wanting to die in the first place. Shoulda kept it in my head until it left me on its own. Now I gotta figure out how to explain it enough to where L.A. ain't making calls and asking further questions, cause "I was playing" ain't never gone cut it.

I don't say nothing bout the boys or brothers, but reiterate what the letter says. I say Banana think I'm fast because I be talking to boys and it come off as if I'm doing more when really I'm doing nothing. That we don't be kissing or touching or having sex because kissing and touching and having sex is what I associate the word to.

"I'm not fast," I say to L.A. I don't mention an older boy, a younger boy, a stanky boy, or a *NeXt* game and how I think I made love with somebody besides her. I talk about boys as a general idea, a theory. Skating rink boys. Cicis Pizza boys. Extended family boys. Swimming pool boys. Astroworld boys. Why boys. How boys. When will boys. Why we gotta deal with boys. Etc. I'm off on many tangents, assuming the semi-suicide letter is about something else entirely. It don't register that all the thoughts have always been threaded.

L.A. nods like she understand where I'm coming from.

Then L.A. tells me to never say I wanna kill myself again because people who kill themselves go to hell. She ain't understanding how I do not care about going to hell. Or that the point always being   here but her always being

there

is also a type of investment.

PART II

BLOOD

I GREW UP IN MY great-great uncle's Southern Baptist church.

- No bare legs
- No pants on women
- No uncrossed ankles
- No questions
- No sex
- No backtalk
- No sitting down
- No matter what
- Sing
- Sing
- Praise
- Praise
- Praise
- PRAISE!!!!
- PRAISE!!!!!!!!! HIM!!!!!!!

Then I stop going the first chance I get.

I can't remember the last time I got on my knees
        to pray
I don't mind the bowing
        it's just I can't stand
all the begging

This the beginning and end of this story.

INCHOIRING MINES

IN MISSIONARY DICTIONARY BAPTIST CHURCH, after finally convincing L.A. to let me get out of the children's choir, I lean my right shoulder against the wall when I know I'm supposed to be standing upright and ushering. It's second Sunday—children's Sunday; and to avoid falling asleep, I stare at all of the chipped-off pieces of white wood that done fell off the wall recently, kicking it into corners full of other broken-off pieces of hair, candy, and cheap clothing. To my left is the pews I'm supposed to be ushering the guests into, but don't nobody be up in here like that so I use what's left of my index fingernail to chip off more of the wood as the choir start singing.

Then I feel the terrible taps on my left shoulder. I already know who it is. Miss Lady. And I know she here to tell me how I ain't doing enough or how I'm doing too much and how I can go about toning it down or picking it up. But whichever it is, is why she takes my elbow and proceeds to pull me toward the restroom at the back of the sanctuary.

When we get inside, it's hard for me not to think of its confines as a cell. It's basically a broom closet with a toilet, but I fight to switch our position, to walk in first; and try not to jerk back my limb as she closes the door with more tenderness than she showed my arm.

By habit, I turn my back to the mirror that's hanging off the door. I don't think I'm ugly but I hate mirrors and cameras even though I'm always smiling and getting in trouble at school for laughing and people love calling me confident, love saying it; and I get confused whether or not I should be proud of my pretending. It's not that I'm confident, it's just I got a problem with authority. Which means I got a problem with the Bible. Which means I got a problem with myself.

I frown, everything on my face droopy like I'm laying upside down because it always smell dingy in here. Wet. Like the entire room on the verge of mildewing or like I'm on the verge of breaking a sweat. Which ima do anyway, usually starting at the tip of my nose and ending at the crease of my back, and I feel it coming on as soon as we enter the space. The only time I voluntarily come in here is when I'm pretending to go blow my nose in order to pass the time of Uncle Needy's slow-speaking sermon. He ain't dead yet, but it's coming; and if he could speed up the speech a lil bit and not . . . spread . . . out . . . every . . . single . . . two . . . syllable . . . word . . . we could get outta here way before he die.

My *why am I here* attitude get on Miss Lady nerves, which is why she look down on me with the same potency she would a woman who borrowing her man.

"Where yo stockings," she say to me, but I don't say nothing cause it ain't nothing to say when I know her eyes work. I don't get why if I'm not bothering nobody, why I always gotta be bothered. But she keep talking. "Now you know you supposed to wear stockings with yo uniform."

Being an usher is worse than sitting in the pew playing MASH with myself while Uncle Needy preaching. I still gotta wear black bottoms and a white collared button-down like I'm a waitress at Pappadeaux. I still gotta show up to *practice* during the week. Shoulda just stayed in the choir, cause now whenever

I wear a skirt of any length—I'm expected to wear stockings too; and I rather do math than wear stockings.

IF IT WAS UP TO me, I wouldn't be doing nothing in the church no more, but ain't no way L.A. gone let that happen. It got sum to do with teaching me what being of service is and I'm thankful for this, but not right now. She still the same, but different now. She talk about church and God being the head of her life all the time and be naming closets to pray in and be singing loud and to the Lord with her palms to the sky but I still be getting whoopings and slapped upside the head for talking back and she a word called *celibate* too even though we only ever listen to horny R&B niggas outside of gospel and she got a crush on Noel Jones and be watching his sermons every night and I tell her that's lusting so I don't know if none of this religion shit be working like she think it do.

Anyways, when she first brought us here I realize we both feel abandoned but both too young to care about expressing it healthily. All we know how to do is surround ourselves with distractions, and before I know it—we at church four days a week and I'm involved in everything a kid can be involved in from this point on. In fact, I get involved in more things to get out of things I no longer wanna be involved in. Christmas plays. Easter poems. Sunday school. Vacation Bible school. Fish fries. Car washes. Choir mostly. But the freedom is an illusion. The only thing they really let kids do in church is sing or stand and sometimes sink and sometimes they make us do all three together at once. I feel like this a lot whenever I'm here throughout the week, but especially on Sundays; like I'm sinking in something I can't even pronounce. Like everybody around keep tryna pull me out by my hands, but my feet won't move.

I join the choir first

even though I can't sing. I'm immediately informed how singing for the Lord is the biggest payback you can give Him, but I feel like this a lie and the real answer is offering. I love to sing loudly for fun though. My cousin Never be saying I sound like Lou Rawls but that's cause sometimes I be forgetting to clear my throat. I don't care though cause I think it's important to enjoy things that don't necessarily reward and praise you. Singing is that. I love songs. Songs are the only thing that makes me feel included and not watched in a *here is where who you are is not enough* way. But I do it so openly, L.A. start thinking me and her having the same church experience. So when I tell her I don't wanna be in the choir no more after everybody fun get grown and leave the church they grew up in, I think it kinda hurt her feelings; the way I know how to hop out of things once they end. And even though I don't believe in us becoming the mother-daughter version of Mary Mary like she hoped, L.A. gone always be L.A., and I don't feel like hearing L.A. mouth, so I knew when I brought up the option to dismiss myself from the choir stand—I needed a plan on what avenue I wanted to venture down next, even if I sometimes read the church announcements on second Sundays when the congregation ain't playing favorites.

& although me and L.A. family, we definitely ain't nobody's favorite.

We just can't help standing out.

It's a difference.

"I AIN'T GOT NONE." I finally say.

Miss Lady stare at me like all the commandments just got broke for stating the obvious. I'm used to her watching me; like most grown women watch me; like they looking for me to pick up they slack, and to start as soon as now. I wish she just say what her problem is cause it ain't entirely about stockings. It's about her not thinking I'm a cute girl, which is fine, since I don't really find her to be that pretty either. She just skinny and stylish and people automatically equate this to beauty. But I equate beauty with freedom and big ol' legs and clear skin and nice teeth so what she think don't really concern me; but she really, really want it to, which is why she tries to fix me. Touch me. Turning my collar back down/giving me lotion for my bare ankles/using her hand as an iron to massage the wrinkles outta my skirt/using her fingers to lead my hair in the direction toward my brain like L.A. ain't did a good enough job getting me ready no days.

You ain't even over the ushers, why you worried about it? is what I really wanna say, but L.A. will lock my arm up for being disrespectful even when I'm being disrespected. If Miss Lady complain enough tho, somebody gone drive up to the beauty supply by the donut shop and get a pair for ninety-nine cents, but all I'ma do is rip a hole in them too same way I did the last pair. It ain't even about being defiant; I make big holes cause them hoes itch.

& holes mean I need mending. I'm not put together enough. I look effortless, and not in the *good-healing big-haired natural-deodorant-wearing earthy-girl* typa way. And none of what I'm not will work in this house of a church. If I've learned anything from this place it's that to be desirable is to be everything and nothing.   Nothing if I'm not.

                Close to nothing if I am. It's why Miss Lady believes her need to dress my kid legs in sexy see-through sequins make sense.

THEY SAY IT'S ALL SPIRITUAL—THE work we think we doing here, but it feel like *spiritual* is code for *sexual*, which they code in all these rules about worshiping A man. The son. The father. Him. The Perfect, Almighty One. I don't know who is actually supposed to be God.

That's why when Gods enter, I gotta stand up

with God's book, to memorize all the scriptures about submission. Gods tell me Mary was a virgin girl who had a baby boy who keeps saving my life. His name is God too. Or Gabriel. I don't be memorizing. I shake hands with them in the front pews and am told to call them by their names. Gods tell me Mary didn't even have sex with her husband and if I wanna be happy—to walk in my true purpose—I need to be Mary who can't be god but who can create him. I ask God how I'm supposed to be a virgin with a husband when I thought I had to have a husband in order to not be a virgin. This god can't answer any of my questions without talking about perception. Another God tells me tradition says women should never wear pants. Every god teaches us to keep our legs closed but teach the mini gods about temptation. Gods say principles only apply to girls. I don't like being a girl,

cause they never ask

if I want a husband or a baby. They gift them to me regardless and sex and love have to mix up like one of my tapes but it sound worse than hell: all these rules you gotta follow in order to be loved and accepted. All these rules you gotta follow to make God care about you. So maybe it ain't the image thing more than it's the wife training thing, the brainwashing thing.

Uncle Needy's wife been dead my whole life. I never even seen a picture of her, but he ain't got no shortage of women tryna be next in line. It's like some of these ladies think who they is, is cultivated by how much status they can garner here with our thirty members. Meaning, if they been making Uncle Needy's plate after church for six years' worth of Sundays, they'll dare another lady to try and scoop up some green beans and Albertsons chicken on a plate before them. And it be trippin me out cause Uncle Needy old. And cheap. And a misogynist. But they don't care. They just want a title. Which means they gotta have the look. Miss Lady is model-esque, and first in line to become a woman who starts all her sentences with "My husband." In this house of a church, she's next in line for family and stability. And this is the story of how I indirectly end up in the restroom getting lectured on my presentation. Me being direct family, they project all of it onto me; this hope that one day I care enough to put the right amount of time and effort into how I look.

I'm generally confused by what it means to be inside of a body, let alone what correctly costuming said body allows you access to. I never thought of beauty as a doorway—as an entry-level position—as a job that can be obtained by anyone. I always thought it was something you either had or you didn't. I didn't think it mattered one way or another. & even if Miss Lady's intentions are purely out of love, we both know this sanctuary is where she peaks. & I know if I had any real desire to mimic her—to satisfy her—to lose those eyes would be awful; to have her legacy destroyed by a preteen's potential and no altar call in sight would devastate her, even if I let her train me.

IT'S NOT TRUE THAT I don't care how I look; it's that I don't like what comes with looking good. With being a walking mural. Since I woke up with *scoot over when I sit down next to you* hips, shit been weird & adult men been commenting on my body ever since.

The men ask me how I'm doing. The men say I'm looking good. The men call me dark & lovely. The men say the girls wasn't made like this back in they day. The men ask my age. The men say I don't look my age. The men are lying. The men say if I was older, nothing would stop them. The men say they can buy me whatever it is I like. The men follow beside me in their cars while I walk. The men try to hook me up with their nephews and sons and brothers. The men ask for my number and say we ain't gotta tell nobody. The men palm the dip of my back at vending machines at L.A.'s job. The men take my palm and place it by their penises. The men stare me down until I'm out of sight. The men never tell other men to stop. & the men in the church ain't no different.

They point out the marks that run up my sides quick like a designer bag. Some of the stretches thicker, darker, like welts from a whip; and some lighter, like my newborn skin, where all lasting things like grief get stored in. I think they see it in my walk.

I stop moving. My hips become my first lost lover.

Of course this is all in the midst of—and after—boys chase girls and girls chase boys and hit each other symbolically. The girl usually starts the chase—push the boy, then run. Once she's caught, neither of them know what to do; so he hits her back and she begins chasing him again.

When the girl chases the boy, she can never catch him.

When the boy chases the girl, she slows down her pace so he can catch up to her.

It's the cycle our childhoods orbit—a sanction where we play pretend with people we think we know.

It never ends. We get older.

We still young. & boys think they know the girls' bodies more than the girls, but are still nice enough to inquire whether or not they can touch whatever has grown. The girls say yes. The girls say no. We get older.

We still young. & now boys are graduating from touching butts timidly to smacking ass regardless of your answer. & girls get in trouble for *letting* them. We get older.

We still young. & boys are getting bigger, braver. Now, boys who was scared to ask what your name is, let alone your number, are getting height. Getting bass. Now, the brave boys we knew to be scared boys be pulling you by the arm behind bleachers. Now, the brave boys we knew to be shy boys be telling you that you know you like it. Now, the brave boys we knew to be sheltered boys think they can tell you what to do and wear and think about yourself. Now, the boys are becoming men.

& they start touching you cause they feel like it. Staring at you across the classroom for no reason. Hitting you cause they ain't got no words. Hitting you cause they can't handle words. Asking you to do stuff for them. They already do it and I'm not even living up to the standard, so I can't imagine how it is for somebody like Miss Lady—the prettiest lady in the whole house—that type of attention would make me skin myself alive. I wish I could ask her why in the world would she ever want this for me, but instead I say, "I'll have the stockings next week!" and run out of the bathroom.

BODY BLOWS

DOLL STANDS IN FRONT OF me and dares me to swing. Whenever we're at his house alone, we fight
                              or work out.

"Okay," he instructs me, "hit here."

I smash my gloveless fist into the cushion of his palm.

One, two.
One, two.

Memorize the combination.

Jab.
        One, two.
Jab.
        One, two.

Duck.

Jab.

Jab.

Duck.

"Most niggas don't work out," he reminds me every time we work out. "Most niggas don't lift or even do push-ups 'nshit like that."

I explain to him, again, how my upper-body strength is non-existent, my Angela Bassett/Tina Turner arms so far out of reach and how me and them niggas he talking bout is in the same boat. But Doll wants me to be strong—like him—cause every-thing else he says is like L.A. So I can't show the pain to him cause we so alike. Doll extremely strong but it's hard to gauge by looking at him. There ain't no bulging muscles poking out of his clothes, or abs, or an abnormally strong neck, or nothing like that. But the boulders are present when he flex, thick as calves. I can't let him think I can't hang. I can't let him know I don't like hitting things. I can't let him think I'm weak even though I got the loosey-goosey arms.

"So you can't do a push-up right now, but get in the push-up position and hold your weight up. Do that every day; you'll get stronger and, boom, pushing out five, ten push-ups at a time."

I ain't finna be doing that every day, but I love how he wanna prepare me for something. Doll takes pride in being productive and practical—not indulgent. He'll cook, clean, mow, plant, or grow whatever it is he needs. I think it got something to do with being self-sufficient or self-absorbed or sum of that nature. Iono. I'm tryna figure it out tho cause I'm the same way; ready to self-teach in order to avoid having to accept help in fear it will be perceived as needing it. As lacking something.

At least that's how I look at it. At least that's what I feel when I throw a punch and he gets amped up, like I'm learning. He thinks

I wouldn't know what to do in a crisis; that I'm privileged and spoiled. It seem like all people do.

"Yo mama got hands. I wouldn't play wit her," he say as I swing, and I laugh and respond with, "Believe me, I know." But I done got good at weaving, which is why me and Doll sparring is just another day.

"You get stronger that way can't no nigga run up on you." Which seems to be the main plot point of my workouts. He a fighter like her, but say he getting too old to knock a nigga out, so he carry his gun. I nod. "You not that tall," Doll observes, "but if you know where to hit, you can knock they ass out." He keep instructing. "It's a few spots that'll get a nigga up off you quick." The nose being the main point. L.A., on the other hand, always tell me, "You karate chop them right here," and point to her throat, "or kick them in they shin. But keep kicking." She add, "Don't stop. You can't let 'em get back up."

Doll points to the crux of the nose we share and say "Aim right here." He grabs my hand and shows me how to properly ball up my fist. "You punch a nigga right here hard enough? I promise you he falling." I nod and practice my fist balling.

"But you ain't gotta worry bout that though." Doll concludes, "If a nigga ever put his hands on you, call me. I don't care how old I am or where I'm at. You can be around the world, I'm coming." I don't really give a verbal answer. I'm too busy wondering how it's possible to feel so protected and unsafe at the same time, but I believe him. I wanna ask more about what he'd do if I was the one to have my hands on a nigga. I nod my head up and down like yeah tho. I jab his hands with my properly folded fist, aim high. I remember him telling me once how if you hit somebody hard enough, it'll hurt you too.

REDMAN AVE

NEVER MOVES INTO A BUILT house.

My house.

Redman Ave.

Brand-new.

One day L.A. say she got a loan to build it—a one-story, two-bath/three-bed in Forney—and takes me to the opening of a cul-de-sac, a lot with nothing but dirt surrounded by two-story homes with white folk inside. We move so much I now look forward to it and building a house feels too permanent. Like I'll never get the chance to leave again. So I ain't that excited about it.

For over a year, we drive back and forth from our apartment to the lot checking on its progression. And although I'm skeptical of its place in my world, the process of building anything interests me enough to pay attention to it. How first, it's just the bottom of the earth: dirt. Then wood.

Then brick.

Then walls.

Then rooms.

Then it gets a name; gets called a home. But I just live here on its outskirts.

THE SUMMER BEFORE I START the fifth grade, we finally move in and L.A. is so proud. So happy. She handpicks all the fixtures and finishes using the leftover commercial loan money. This is her thing—coordinating. Even her clothes say color and intention. She ain't never seen two of them as tacky. If you point out confliction, she looks genuinely confused by the statement and always responds with "They solid colors."

Everybody keep talking bout how the house is so nice because we got two living rooms but I think it's too much space. I go from sharing a bed with L.A. to a bunk bed with L.A. to getting my own room and don't know what to do with it, how to thrive in it, so I rip out all the posters from my *Word Up!* and *J-14* magazines; forming my name on the wall out of them with thumbtacks and scotch tape. I don't think my mind has time to care about the aesthetics of stuff because it's too busy thinking about getting away and entering the future, so I'm never really aware of what's presently happening and what it'll mean. It look like decorations, but really it's about territory. I dream of land. Of smaller packaged space. Of stars. Of quiet. Of weekends at home for once with no extra visitors. & for a few months, I get it; a dog, dinners, and doors to close.

Then we go get Never.

HE BEEN CLIMBING OUT OF windows at night to meet up with some girl. She white. They keep bringing this up as the reason he acting reckless, but I heard Doll say once that recklessness is what's bound to happen when boys get they first piece of pussy. That there ain't no length they won't go in order to keep getting it, and I think even a broke clock is right twice a day.

Never's length is impressing the girl with gifts he ain't buy on nights when he supposed to be home & other normal teenage things teenagers do when they feel the rush of deep like. The lengths he go ain't seen as romantic though and end up getting him kicked out of where he's lived for almost a decade during his junior year of high school.

Because L.A. is the first call our family always makes—when she gets this one, we pull up to my uncle's front door the same day all because L.A. loooooooves Never and thinks he can do no irreversible wrong even when he do her wrong. L.A. never say he got a takeover spirit tho, cause he her favorite nephew even if she say she ain't got no favorites and treat everybody the same, but this only half true. She do treat everybody the same; but as a family favorite myself—I know it's levels to what she tolerates depending on who doing what—which is why she don't ask no questions but got me helping him put his bags in the trunk.

When Never tries to get into the car without saying bye, our uncle stops him.

"Hey man," he says to his back. "You not gone say bye?" He means thank you. "You been here this long," he reminds him the midst of his evacuation, "and you not gone say bye?"

A thank-you is definitely warranted, but a grand one seems a bit much for my taste seeing as how Never is a kid I'm constantly in conversation with. Since our birthdays are one day apart, our family always say that so many disagreements happen between me and him because we so alike, from the skin to the soul to the secrecy. That we both think we know everything. That our tones are off, our delivery be wrong. That we clash because we the same, even though I've never believed in opposites attracting. And it's been ingrained in me so it's hard to not put myself in his shoes.

I don't know what it feels like to be kicked out. But I'm sure it all is making Never feel as if he got got because I'm feeling the same way. Even at twelve, or ten, I can see this. Can identify loss. It's different from a gaping hole of leaking blood. I know blood dries up, ceases at some point once you run out of insides. This is about the despair that follows the disregard of not being good enough to be pardoned—or kept—which makes it hard for trust to ever really enter into the picture, let alone gratitude.

I look from our uncle to L.A., who looks on just the same to Never and back again. It's like I'm always . . . there. Somewhere unnoticed; unchartered. I look up at them, learning the best way to communicate in these types of situations is to say nothing. It don't be mattering. We both know what's being said is filler anyway and won't change the outcome of him having to get the hell out of his house. Staying silent is the only concrete way you get to leave with a lil bit of dignity.

Never turns around, gives our uncle a barely there hug and I realize he's growing. That he's not a kid like me, but a teenager. How we used to be the same height for a long time, but now the white tall tee twelve times his size is seemingly shorter. How when we were younger, they used to make us stand back to back in order to laugh at his smallness—our similar-ness, but now the gap has widened. How he ain't technically tall, but looks his age now. How they'd never let us share a bed. How I thought a new start was the point of our new house, but L.A. keep repeating old patterns. How she feels so sorry for him not being close to his mother/ her sister that now all she wanna do is influence him since they've both been so hurt by her. How she don't have a sentence's worth of conversation with me about Never moving in. How I don't expect her to have a conversation with me about who lives with us. How I don't expect my *no* to be honored in any way. How I don't know if I would even say no in the first place when he just a kid. How family is family. How this is how it is I guess. How the back room we had other plans for becomes his. How the hall bathroom becomes ours. How L.A. gets to save everybody else's children again. How she can't wait for them to share more things. How her eyes light up just looking at him. How they never been closer.

NEVERLAND

I TELL HIM HOW WHEN I finally got out the bed that morning, Never wasn't moving, so it's easy to see why I thought he was still sleep. How this is when I got confused and my knowing began to feel like my imagination but I practically prance out of the bedroom and into the bathroom at the end of the hall. How I wash my hands nonstop for what feels like over an hour, packing bar soap on top of hand soap, over and over again; leaving the faucet off until I'm ready to rinse.

Then repeat the process. How I was hoping

—waiting, really—that somebody else in the house would wake up.

I tell him how they don't. How it must've been really, really early. How I missed L.A. a lot. How I kept scrubbing until my knuckle skin started stinging, same way my fingers do when I bite the skin down too far. That I started biting my nails down to the white meat; but so does Doll so I thought it was inherited. How I don't look in the mirror once. How I stand at the sink and assume the tingling in my palms is because of all the dirt on my hands. How it won't go down the drain. How I rub them together, brush them against one another until they start to squeak. How I can't stop thinking about bacteria. How I think I'm a bad person who hurts people without knowing. How I only accept nobody is

gone come once there's no more soap to use. How I think I'm supposed to be crying but I don't know how to. How I wanna bleed.
How I rather bleed. How without blood, I got no evidence. How
I'm sorry for wasting time saying the same things. How I'm so
sorry. How I know we already talked about this. How if I'm being real, Never is the closest male relationship I've ever had in my
life and that ain't really saying much at all. How if this is *close*, I
don't really know what to say about my life. How sometimes I feel
like I'm the only one who can talk negatively about him. How I
always think what would've happened if my body wasn't trained
to wake up so early in the mornings. How memory, I think, has
made a mummy out of me. Or a man. How this point makes
him start writing things down in the notepad again while I sit
there looking dumb. How I imagine he's writing down the word
AVOIDANCE followed by my symptoms: dismis-
sive,

> stubborn,
> closed off,
> self-aware,
> to the point of performance,
> in pain
> and not able to process it
since she's unaware of its presence,   sure,

after I say "It can't be molestation." How it *can't* be molestation because that would mean too many other things now have
a name.

"What would you call it? It ain't rape either, so do I even got
the right to make a production out of it now? It's just a penis."

How I went back in the room after I used up all the soap. How
Never still wasn't moving. How the only thing different is he had
turned around the other way to face the door, so when I walked
back in and saw he was knocked out, I really thought I was going

crazy. How I walked back around the bottom of the bed to the side I slept on and stood there looking at it, at his back. How it felt like a trick. How I looked around, observing my surroundings, accessing my escape plan. How I got back in the bed.

How Never don't move once, his body deadweight. How I don't even think he breathing. How I lay as close to the edge of my side as I can get, my back toward him too; the same position I woke up in. How I'm so close to the edge, if I breathe too hard, I might fall right out of it. How I know if he rolls back over—if he makes any sudden movement, I can buy myself some time to swing back, or hit the floor.

"Maybe I did dream it though," I finish for the second time, "cause when I opened my eyes, all I kept hearing was L.A. in my head saying *Boys got penises and girls got vaginas* and how her voice is the thing that brought me into consciousness." How her voice made my eyes shoot open. How hearing her in my head is the only reason I recognized what was in my hand without seeing what was in my hand. How she always said *And don't let nobody touch it.*

COMING OF AGE

IT'S AN EMBARRASSING CORRELATION, BUT one summer L.A. sends me this book length text about how she feels I'm being sneaky and hiding things from her when all she's tryna do is make sure I'm safe around the people I'm with and how I don't even call her while I'm in Houston for months and when I do I'm acting like I'm in a rush to get off of the phone and sometimes she feels sick at the thought of other people touching me and I'm sixteen and six and the longer I read the madder I get so I start to cry only because I'm exhausted that I gotta be everybody's parent and I'm too scared to cry in the light so I touch myself at midnight under Doll's roof and think about sounds to stop myself from spiraling and this is the only way I know how because sex and shame in myself has become a lifeline I've been conditioned to be good at and sex and shame with myself is the only thing I got that I can control so I use my fingers to slide across the slit between my thighs and I'm sweating but even under the covers I feel watched as an involuntary tear pops once things feel good and I get scared and think I'll turn into a pool and then into a different person who can't stop crying even though I desperately wanna do so but I lay very still instead even though I'm almost seventeen or seven it's easy to be I'm late for everything and everything I do that's been worth it I've done

last minute cause I tend to learn so
much about myself in the panic and I touch myself wholly meaning I put both hands over me for protection from myself since
they can't fit in me and lay very still as if any sudden movement
will proceed in my door being opened and me being caught and
I turn everything into a survival tactic but that's how I master it
cause anything that wants to progress, will

> Like how at first it's my hand
>
> Then the shower faucet
>
> Then you hate yourself
>
> Then it's [INSERT OBJECT HERE]
>
> Then you remember you can cry, you can feel
>
> Then you hate yourself because it takes so much
> > to feel
>
> Then you punishing yourself for feeling but
> > you can't stop
>
> because overstimulation is the only way it feel like you
> > won't disperse into your bloodline
>
> Then it's hours on the floor in a locked closet
>
> Then you hate yourself
>
> Then it becomes the only way you can cry
>
> And it becomes a conversation
>
> Then a secret
>
> Then humiliation
>
> Then a lie

Then it's just your life and it happens so fast and it
happens so loudly and you form a lot of habits and cry under
covers in houses you don't belong in while trying to see if there's
a difference between crying and coming and how once, you ask
your mama if ya'll can go to therapy together
because you think maybe ya'll are too codependent and she looks
at you like you just said your cousin touched you in a spot they

shouldn't have because she can't understand what it is to discuss when she's your best friend and you hate yourself so of course you try to outdo yourself and it's not as hard as everyone may think and everyone thinks you're the loveliest most secure girl in the world because you do things well and still manage to be kind about it and once you do it so long you wish you could tell some-body how the legs don't necessarily shake more than they stiffen

   Like a shiver when the temperature drops without

    warning

   A knee-jerk reaction

   A sneeze you been waiting all day to blow

   Or whiplash

   How you've made yourself   stop

breathing. And when you go to wipe. You see blood. You open yourself. For yourself. It's how you know nothing. That is yours. Could ever be taken. Even if you gotta cry through it. How you inhale through it. Since life is about breathing. How you wonder if this is why we always break. How sometimes you think what if you die like this. Found lifeless with your eyes rolled into the back of your head. Your fingers stiff. Your blood uncirculated. Your mind blown from too much triggering. How you wonder what lie would be created to cover up who you are one last time. And you hate yourself but when you do things well, you forget. And you love yourself, you really love yourself, for your brain, mostly. And they look to you for all the answers, even though you only four years old. & you don't know how to say you barely a shell when they love you for having so much fun.

PICK

"OKAY. THREE PEOPLE IN THE family to be stuck on an island with, who you picking?" L.A. ask.

"Uhhhh . . ." I already know my answer, but I kick up dirt to make it look like I tried to think harder about it. "You. Lateral. And uhhhh . . . Granny."

"Why?"

"Cause if I'm finna die, I wanna laugh."

"Okay. Okay." She moves on. "Would you rather be invisible or read people's minds?"

"Invisible. Easily."

"A nice wedding or a nice honeymoon?"

"Umm . . ." I don't know how I feel about marriage and me, but I fall in love in five-minute increments all the time, so I say "Honeymoon."

"Where?"

"Iono. Far."

"For a million dollars, if you had to kiss Flavor Flav . . ."

"Nope." I cut her off. Too far.

"A million dollars?!" she ask me again like I ain't hear her the first time. For the sake of the game, I guess. I get quiet. I gotta think this through. I ask the important questions first.

"Open or closed mouth?"

She respond too quick. "Open."

I wasn't ready. It feel like a setup. Like I'm being used for a sound bite.

"Okay den." I stall. Start hopping around in place. "Okay. Okay, okay, okay." I spin in circles to think. "Aw man. Tongue or no tongue?"

"What?"

"Huh?"

She roll her eyes.

"Whatchu think for a million dollars."

This decision hurts cause I'd like to think it's a lot of things I won't do for a million dollars, but this ain't one of 'em.

"Okay. Okay . . . Is this million in cash?"

"Girl, if you don't answer this question. Yes. In cash."

"I'ma say . . . I'ma say yeah bro."

She sitting here laughing at my shame.

"What bout you?" I flip it. I gotta get the thought outta my head. "Same question."

"I ain't doing it," she tell me. "I don't care how much money you gone give me. Baby, naw." First of all, she is lying; but I hate playing games or making bets with L.A., cause she stay

reneging. Every single time.

"You said I gotta pick!!!" I respond, every single time. "Flavor Flav got a good personality though!" I say to try and convince her I make quality decisions. I know she just using these questions to access what I like. Who I am. Whether I've changed. What I've experienced as I'm growing up and out. She seen the show. She know what I mean when I say, "He funny!" But my quality decision making got me bent over laughing too.

"Girl, naw. I don't care what he is, I ain't gone be able to do it." L.A. always talking bout how she gotta be attracted to a man regardless of who he is and what he got cause eventually they all act a fool so the least they can do is be cute. She tell me even all her old boyfriends was at least cute growing up, even if she wasn't sure if she really liked any of them forreal or if they was just there. Say she even had a boyfriend who got killed, and when I ask how that was as a pivotal moment of her life—she say she don't even think she cried. She tells me how on her prom night, she had a boyfriend who left her on the side of the road cause she ain't wanna go to a motel with him and how in '84 she "quit" her boyfriend after he took his homeboy to the Janet Jackson concert instead of her—and I nod, cause, same; but that she moved on and ain't really miss none of them.

She say whenever boys would knock on Granny door back in the gap looking for her or her sister, Granny would slam the door real hard in they face and not even tell them somebody was ever there. That they'd find out the next day at school when somebody say "Ya'll mama mean." And that make me laugh cause Granny is mean to men; but that's my favorite thing about her. L.A. can be mean to men too, but it come way later. At first, she just wanna be loved.

We move so much that boys ain't never got no time to figure out where it is I stay, so I can't relate but it sound fun. L.A. say that don't matter. Proximity ain't never stopped no show; that if somebody really want you, you ain't gone have to wonder if they want you cause they gone always find a way to get to you. Sometimes what people say got precautions in it that trump what they do; like little caveats that can help you avoid going through it. I listen closely to all advice, even if I don't fully agree. L.A. say if you ever gotta guess, and especially if you gotta ask—the answer is no; and not to ever disrespect yourself by asking. Just go on about yo business.

"You kissed somebody yet?" This the real question she been waiting to ask. I knew it was a setup. I'm fourteen. Maybe twelve.

Prolly thirteen. And all I hear is my homegirl in my head saying how we supposed to be kissing in middle school and saving sex for high school, even though a lot of my friends are already doing both.

"Yeah," I don't lie

but I do omit the *all the time*, the *every day*, that is sitting in my throat.

"WHO you done kissed?!" It's a trick question. She already know the answer. I just won't confirm it. If I say who we know it is, she gone assume I'm doing more than kissing cause although we the same age, the boy I been kissing look bout twenty.

I say another name.

"Chain." A nicer boy. A cuter boy. More my speed. A boy who I ain't never did more than give a church hug to and let sing me a Chris Brown song.

"Mmm-hmm . . ." she say, semi-proud of my fake answer, I think. "I used to love kissing. I could kiss all day." And I look up at her with a scrunched-up face, cause the way she falls back into something with only a thought makes me uncomfortable, but also makes me realize either

I don't love kissing like that

can't kiss

got weak jaws

or been kissing the wrong

person.

[HEARTBREAK!]
HAND-ME-DOWNS

I'M FOURTEEN AND [HEARTBREAK!] NEVER walks to school with us more than we walk *from* school together. I'm fourteen and the long, winding, raggedy cement road on the other side of traffic that we ease on down leads to Maynard H. Jackson. I'm fourteen and it's encapsulated the last five years of our lives; switching from elementary into a middle school and houses all of our best days. I'm fourteen and since we been kept together longer than expected, we feel like a family. I'm fourteen and today [Heartbreak!] acting like we just met. I'm fourteen and all of a sudden; the pattern we spent years mapping out needs to be guided. I'm fourteen and we pass through the lot and past Good Luck, where we buy link sandwiches and milkshakes after school. I'm fourteen and [Heartbreak!] looks both ways for everyone before screaming at us to go. I'm fourteen and we don't care if cars are coming or not—we break free from one another and haul ass across the double-sided street. I'm fourteen and horns honk as we run crookedly across. I'm fourteen and nobody is afraid of dying. I'm fourteen and we learning what it mean to be front row and frantic, in a secondary state of fearlessness and fragility. I'm fourteen and [Heartbreak!] gives cars the finger cause it's nothing weighing him down in this moment—not a backpack or a pencil in sight, but his knuckles are always bruised. I'm fourteen and we race but I'm last because, running. I'm fourteen and these are our last days together. I'm fourteen and it's kinda perfect, the end; but don't nobody wanna admit it. I'm fourteen and [Heartbreak!] on me more than usual; not literally, but in a complimentary way. I'm fourteen and we don't be holding hands but he be holding on to me. I'm fourteen and find it weird since I ain't even answer the phone for him last night. I'm fourteen and we walk in the middle of roads because they ours; I dance in streets; I hesitate; I run. I'm fourteen and a woman dropping off her kids yells out of her window "Get yo apple-head ass out the street!" and my friends die laughing. I'm fourteen and I think these types of happenings are the reason [Heartbreak!] think he love me for the moment. I'm fourteen and [Heartbreak!] pulls me back by my arm so I won't get hurt. I'm fourteen and he keep mistaking my impulsiveness for being honest. Or free. I don't know. I'm fourteen; & we don't know how reckless it can get because we fourteen. I'm fourteen and [Heartbreak!] telling my friend something about love with my name in the middle loud enough for me to hear even though next year she'll tell me how he try to holla once I go to a different high school. I'm fourteen and I roll my eyes outta the sockets and push his arm to alert him to hush. I'm fourteen and love kinda embarrassing, even if I feel it. I'm fourteen and my friend is laughing cause I lied and told her I never say it back even if it took me a long time to do so. I'm fourteen and he said it after one week but he always been a liar. I'm fourteen and that was almost two years ago. I'm fourteen and he done said it so much he convinced himself he do. I'm fourteen and sum feels off; he being way too nice, when our kinda nice is "witcho apple-head ass," not no "you look good today."

I'M FOURTEEN WHEN MY FRIEND stands directly in front of me and asks have I seen [Heartbreak's!] neck. I'm fourteen and we all got gym eighth period. I'm fourteen and she sits down in the empty desk right next to me. I'm fourteen and I say "naw" cause I haven't seen his neck. I'm fourteen and [Heartbreak!] playing floor hockey like he getting paid for it, swinging the stick with a power that's semi-funny considering the effort of everybody else playing. I'm fourteen and I know whatever he tries, he good at: football, running, hiding, drawing, paying attention. I'm fourteen and I see him see what's happening cause he drops his hockey stick and approaches us, or me, I don't know, I'm fourteen and I immediately get the impression that everybody but me already know about whatever it is my friend is referring to. I'm fourteen and with every step [Heartbreak!] takes toward us, it comes clearer and bigger until the thing on his neck looks like a birthmark. I'm fourteen and asking myself how didn't I see it this morning and why don't I pay attention to other people's bodies the way I need to, especially the bodies close to my own. I'm fourteen and once he in front of me, I raise his chin like he's my child. I'm fourteen and the imprint blends flawlessly into the flesh between his clavicle and Adam's apple. It's some nice skin. Smooth. Shaded in a sweet violet undertone. Shaped like a lop-sided heart. I'm fourteen and I wanna wipe out his windpipe. At least collapse its entryway and watch him suffocate. I'm fourteen and I don't got much experience with boys, but I done had enough run-ins with men to know the games ain't that different. I'm fourteen and I believe in him starting young; how it's a type of molding. A crowning. I'm fourteen and I let my hand fall from his face. I'm fourteen and I tell him "You can go." I'm fourteen and he sucks his teeth like I'm getting on his nerves. I'm fourteen but he backs away.

I'M FOURTEEN AND FOR THE rest of our gym period [Heartbreak!]
sends all our mutual friends over to explain his hickey but I done
took off my ears. I'm fourteen and when the bell rings our coaches
push us out the back door like roaches and we start our journey
back across the field. I'm fourteen and as long as we been around,
the grass ain't never been alive; it'll never be nothing more than a
shortcut we take to get back to the street, to get back to Good Luck.
I'm fourteen, and what always starts off as a mob of us usually dis-
perses into our core group. I'm fourteen and I ain't said nothing
to nobody since seeing and somebody say plain and dry, "She mad
cause you keep lying." I'm fourteen and don't know why I'm mad.
I'm fourteen and he start pulling on my arm and mentions not lying.
I'm fourteen and touch makes me open my mouth more than whatever else I'm supposed to be processing. I'm fourteen and I say "Let
me go bro," and continue to walk away from the group. I'm fourteen
and I don't think any of them have ever seen me upset so they don't
know what to do. I'm fourteen and I find myself searching for safety
and solitude and sugar. I'm fourteen and [Heartbreak!] who ain't
never offered to buy me nothing since I been knowing him tries
to pay for my milkshake. I'm fourteen and decline his money but I
keep all the gifts and other things he's made me: rosaries and letters
and self-portraits and rings. I'm fourteen and try to walk past him
with my stuff but he grabs me and won't let me move. I'm fourteen
and part of me stands there to see who he lies like. I'm fourteen and
the answer is nobody special. I'm fourteen and I didn't know feelings that took so long to develop could die in one conversation. I'm
fourteen and the next day after school, I sit around talking to my
favorite teacher to avoid the field. I'm fourteen when she laugh and
say, "I saw you and [Heartbreak!] fighting in the field yesterday."
I'm fourteen and I press my thumb to my forehead, shake my head,
and laugh too. But really I'm bout to cry.

I'M FOURTEEN AND [HEARTBREAK!] ALWAYS on a lot of girl's minds, but mostly mine. I'm fourteen and everybody in the school know I'm capable but just a girl. I'm fourteen and I don't believe in being in love but I be telling him I love him sometimes. I'm fourteen and I use the signature *Kendra & [Heartbreak!]* after every text I send to him, but not to nobody else cause I'm ashamed after they know things. I'm fourteen and [Heartbreak!] say he waited in the rain for me and I never showed and I coulda at least told him I wasn't coming. I'm fourteen and I don't really give a damn about his feelings once he walks me to school with a hickey from another girl on his neck. I'm fourteen and if you hurt my feelings, I'm gone make you feel it. I'm fourteen and I sit on his lap during the last week of school and he thinks I forgave him but I'm already plotting on disappearing from his life. I'm fourteen and "Complicated" by Nivea is my Myspace song because I'm dramatic. I'm fourteen and "Complicated" by Avril Lavigne is his ringtone because I'm clear. I'm fourteen and I don't see the point in claiming niggas so I don't. I'm fourteen and we broke up; but I see him at the fair with way too many people, and he stops everyone's walk to look at me differently when I'm outside of my school clothes. I'm fourteen and he grabs my mouth, admires my teeth and lips and face, and no matter what, is always proud of me. I'm fourteen and he buys me an ice cream as an apology but I let the cream melt down my knuckles cause I'm still mad. I'm fourteen and I never lick my wounds. I'm fourteen and never had a hickey. I'm fourteen and he looks me dead in the face and tells me it's not a hickey on his neck. I'm fourteen and he's fourteen and can't tell good lies but knows how to stick to his story. I'm fourteen and wanna fight multiple men. I'm fourteen and [Heartbreak!] is ready to fight over me when another boy treats me better than he does. I'm fourteen and grasp how everyone who says they love me swings first. I'm fourteen and I'm already over this boy/girl shit, it's boring. I'm fourteen and he touches my legs under the table of our eighth-grade prom. I'm fourteen and finally over him, but it ain't hit him yet. I'm fourteen and he looks up and I look down and I want touch, but I don't know from who.

I'M FOURTEEN AND WE SPEND more time together now than we did then even though he's not waiting outside for me after school no more. I'm fourteen and he's picking me up, spinning me around, and setting me down on the green high-voltage box outside the gym. I'm fourteen and he didn't come to school today because he got sent to an alternative school for six weeks. I'm fourteen and he's showing up for the new girl who transferred to our school like five days ago. I'm fourteen and they "go together." I'm fourteen and he got her same way he got me. I'm fourteen and we both wait on different people. I'm fourteen and he stands over me not as a declaration of possession, but to show off how excessive he can be. I'm fourteen and he tells me *I always miss you* while we wait on different things. I'm fourteen and I'll never feel this good and this bad at once again. I'm fourteen and remembering how L.A. told me heartbreak is the worst pain she's ever felt. I'm fourteen and me or L.A. don't even know I'm heartbroken. I'm fourteen and sneaking to read his letter under a textbook during computer class. I'm fourteen and he says I'm the one keep breaking up with him. I'm fourteen and he promises not to hurt me again. I'm fourteen and lowkey offended he got the audacity to think I'd let him do it twice. I'm fourteen and he says he hopes we still together before telling me we gone always be together. I'm fourteen and Mr. Hen and Ms. Win tell me rings and thangs is a move to get the panty drawls and I better not be giving [Heartbreak!] no nothing. I'm fourteen and my friends keep reassuring me I can have [Heartbreak!] whenever I want and I ask them to please stop talking to me cause that's not the compliment they think it is. I'm fourteen when the new girl makes space to tell the entire classroom that [Heartbreak!] already said he loves her and that they're forever. I'm fourteen and this kid shit should feel more kid-friendly. I'm fourteen and

I'm not mad at her or him. I'm fourteen and he hands me what I think is another letter as we pass through the halls to our next period. I'm fourteen and it's not a letter but a picture he drew of himself with my first name accompanied by his last name inside of a heart that I'll keep as a memory but not for a sentiment. I'm fourteen and tired of things that aren't certain. I'm fourteen and this back-and-forth shit is for the birds. I'm fourteen and his new girl finally comes out of the gym door and he hugs me bye right in front of her. I'm fourteen and I learn my lessons the first time. I'm fourteen and I never see his penis but I be hearing a lot about it. I'm fourteen and I know I'm getting fucked, but not in the same way she about to be.

I'M THIRTEEN AND ALL CHRISTMAS break [Heartbreak!] keep asking me will he be my first. I'm thirteen and Doll snatches my phone out of my hand and reads all the texts of me lying and saying yeah. I'm thirteen and Doll don't speak to me until nighttime, the next day. I'm thirteen and Doll talks to me about boys being transactional instead of talking to me about who he is. I'm thirteen and before I go to softball practice, I meet [Heartbreak!] behind one of the ISS portables. I'm thirteen and my cousin Candy's nickname for me is A-Cup. I'm thirteen and I know affection, but I still need assistance with hand stuff. I'm thirteen and I'm nervous about nipple hair. I'm thirteen and I rest my back against the portable slack as [Heartbreak!] takes my barely there breasts out of my sports bra and sucks, same way I would've that ice cream cone. I'm thirteen and I'm staring at a blank wall waiting to feel something better, but I only feel nine. I'm thirteen and scared about getting caught, but it feels good outside. I'm thirteen and I move his mouth around anyway and watch him turn into my baby. I'm thirteen and I lose things for him. I'm thirteen when a boy in class catches my attention and grabs at his own A-cups and pretends to lick. I'm thirteen and I get convenient. I'm thirteen and deny like a man. I'm thirteen when I start reminding myself of my father. I'm thirteen and [Heartbreak!] and I win most popular but not most compatible. I'm thirteen and he gets mad at me for rating Chain a ten and him a nine on the *finest boys in our grade* list that's going around. I'm thirteen and he don't understand I was ranking looks, not prominence. I'm thirteen and [Heartbreak!]'s never been mean to me but sometimes we still treat each other poorly. I'm thirteen but I think him and I make each other feel definite.

I'M THIRTEEN AND [HEARTBREAK!] TEXTS me the lyrics to a Plies song after I break up with him again. I'm thirteen and the text says "you can be stupid and give me away if you want to," like I don't know he texting me the lyrics to a Plies song. I'm thirteen and respond quickly to threats. I'm thirteen and can feel Chain staring at me from across the gym floor during a basketball game. I'm thirteen when a chain message goes around about revealing a year-end secret to the sender and Chain replies with *I love you* but I panic because he's not [Heartbreak!]. I'm thirteen and [Heartbreak!] ask why would he ask me to put myself all over his Myspace page if I wasn't the only one he loved. I'm thirteen when I say I ain't finna do all that and read all his messages instead. I'm thirteen when my algebra teacher separates me from [Heartbreak's!] lips outside of his classroom after the bell for fifth period rings. I'm thirteen when I start reminding myself of my mother. I'm thirteen and [Heartbreak!] breaks up with me for the first and only time. I'm thirteen and I'm avoiding him because ain't nothing to talk about and he's avoiding me because he got back with ol' girl. I'm thirteen and keep tryna manifest him through my thoughts, hoping it'll make him text me. I'm thirteen and sitting in church while Never is using my phone to text that white girl when he does. I'm thirteen when Never reads the texts before I do and ask me if [Heartbreak!] is my boyfriend or sum while laughing at whatever he read. I'm thirteen and would rather die than have him knowing my heart feels. I'm thirteen and snatch my phone back outta his hand; tell him don't worry bout me and what I'm doing when he need to be worried bout getting his line up fixed.

I'M THIRTEEN AND IN *LOVE* wit [Heartbreak!] but apprehensive about believing it because I already know the outcome of love. I'm thirteen and he start acting like I'm the only girl in the world. I'm thirteen and L.A. say she hope I don't think I got a boyfriend after he posts up in her car window and calls her his mother-in-law. I'm thirteen and he says every time he hears "Suffocate" he thinks of me because he knows it's my favorite song. I'm thirteen and this nigga got a lil bit of game. I'm thirteen and he definitely having sex, just not with me. I'm thirteen and these boys I'm dealing with sense something in me I can't pronounce. I'm thirteen and got three boyfriends. I'm thirteen and I lie to [Heartbreak!] about kissing Low in the back of computer class when he was away at alternative school. I'm thirteen and I only kiss Low once, but it feel way better than kissing him. I'm thirteen and I can't stop thinking bout it. I'm thirteen and I really like Low but I do him wrong and stop talking to him once [Heartbreak!] returns. I'm thirteen and I take it back—[Heartbreak!] don't got game, I'm just dumb. I'm thirteen and I know that none of this really counts but it feels like [Heartbreak!] has to. I'm thirteen and learning a type of tolerance I wish it wasn't so easy to adapt to. I'm thirteen and a boy I like makes me cry for the only time. I'm thirteen when I make Chain sing "Yo" after English class and this is how we start going together. I'm thirteen and we look good on paper and I should like him more but I already like [Heartbreak!]. I'm thirteen and me and his relationship is a bunch of hugs throughout the day. I'm thirteen and he is debatably the cutest boy in our grade and we like each other but that's not enough. I'm thirteen and don't respect nothing that make me wait unnecessarily and he shouldn't have to either. I'm thirteen and have my first kiss in the back cubicle of Mr. Hen's class after school. I'm thirteen and [Heartbreak!] leads me into the room on purpose. I'm thirteen when my friend insinuates how I'm already acting like I'm having sex with him. I'm thirteen and I hear Banana's voice in my head. I'm thirteen and don't know what I'm doing. I'm thirteen but I still wear [Heartbreak!]'s ID badge around my neck and his ring around my finger. I'm thirteen and his lips were chapped. He kept his tongue in his mouth. It wasn't special. I never assumed it'd be. I didn't feel different. He smiled real sneaky.

I'M TWELVE AND I KNOW who [Heartbreak!] is but I don't know what he'll mean. I'm twelve and already taking my choices way too seriously to the point where I rarely choose. I'm twelve and my first fake boyfriend is a black boy with red hair. I'm twelve and our entire class is surprised; not because they all liked him, but because I like him. I'm twelve and he's clearly a good, nice boy; almost too innocent. I'm twelve and I make him jump through hoops before I sit with him at lunch. I'm twelve and I feel a hundred eyes on my back. I'm twelve and already hate people in my business. I'm twelve and he texts me to *ask* if he can kiss me tomorrow after school. I'm twelve and it just never happens because I don't want it to happen. I'm twelve and [Heartbreak!] sits across from me at the lunch table while sitting next to another girl. I'm twelve and not stupid. I'm twelve and they go together but I don't care cause I don't feel. I'm twelve and I know [Heartbreak!] really likes me cause I'm always catching him staring with the best eyes. I'm twelve and he tells a friend to tell me that he likes me. I'm twelve and I know [Heartbreak!] is a hothead with a nice face. I'm twelve and I ain't thinking bout no boys, let alone waiting for them to see me. I'm twelve and the only thing I'm sure of is how afraid I am of them. I'm twelve and it's hard to explain or excuse, but this fear I got is what lets me know I have to try.

LASSO A LINEAGE

"1999" by Prince prolly played in the background somewhere and I turned five. On December 30 of that same year, Granddaddy died

of everything. Liver and lung cancer mostly; but a lil bit of all the cancers lived and died in him too. If I claimed to be a writer then, his obituary would read he lived round the way, about forty-five minutes west of L.A. and her siblings, drunk to death on a porch, and got along well with my father. Between the Korean War and alcoholism, I don't know what to call it all. Maybe the war outweighs the alcoholism or is it the same thing. Maybe the alcoholism is a symptom of the war, or are we all the same things, only learning how to sink in order to temporarily absolve ourselves of the weight. Lean is the family name. I'm one of the few people without it but I'm it. Anyways, most people called Granddaddy "Pig." And most formally—Pigalee. Which still don't explain why I grew up thinking Granddaddy was Jerome from *Martin*, but I did—until I was about ten, I thought of him a mack-daddy type with young-adult girlfriends. The only way I could remember him alive was with a tight curl shining from all that grease and a gold tooth accompanied by a color-coordinated—sometimes animal-printed—ensemble. In actuality, I never got to know him good enough to remember full details of his face, let alone know him at all to be writing about it. But I know he had none of this slip, and most likely it was the beard connecting him and Jerome's temperaments in my mind; but it felt right to assume, and sometimes still to imagine— it's all there is to do.

Anyways, again, I wore a murky velvet dress to his funeral and fell asleep in my father's lap.

When he was alive, I remember us sitting outside way more, lining his duplex with lawn chairs to stare out into the field of dirt they keep describing as a yard. He was said to be a sunup-to-sundown kinda addict: lazy laying and liquor and lying. One time while we sat in them lawn chairs, Granddaddy told my daddy, Doll, he need to slap L.A. so she can shut up sometimes like her name was Ms. Sofia or sum. L.A. told her daddy her husband ain't no drunk woman beater like him. I guess not being a woman beater is good enough.

If him and Jerome shared anything, it was looking hud out and having a big mouth. I know, cause most of us talk first and ask questions later. Most of us always got something to get off our chests. Most of us always tryna get over a hump. We had to get it from somewhere, and Granny sits even-toned and to the point.

HIM AND HER MET IN high school. They wasn't sweethearts. Granny was a student and Granddaddy was the janitor. It seems as if someone would infiltrate, the age gap predatory and doomed, but there ain't no consequence for snatching up the Black youth. He sweet-talked her right out her mama's house and right into marriage—twenty years her senior. When he died, they'd been long divorced, and he said although he truly loved her, he had to go because she wouldn't stop having all them kids.

Granny ended up raising their four kids during the seventies with no daddy. I only mention it because people tend to think it matters. I used to think so too; but Granny raised their four kids during the seventies with no money, and this way worse than no daddy. They lived in Oak Cliff, a neighborhood in Dallas that extends through four generations of our women. Granny raised hers all high as the streetlights and when they came on around six thirty every night—they had better been back in the house whether she was home or not. The streetlight—I'm told—is the indicator of tardiness in times where other time-telling options weren't an option. The streetlight a yell. A responsibility. Another warning.

WHEN GRANDDADDY BEGAN BEATING GRANNY, she was forever young. When L.A. was three—their third-born child—she saw her daddy slap her mama in the kitchen. The same day, L.A. had her first Fig Newton when she went to their neighbor's house and confessed what had happened was . . . & the neighbor gave her the tart cause she ain't know what to say. That's how it always be. Grown folk proposition and beg kids to tell them the things their bodies went through and never know what to do with the information except for pacify you with sweets and sometimes kisses. L.A. say bout a year later, Granny divorced Granddaddy. That each time she would attempt to leave before, her mother—my great-grandmother—would tell her to go back home to her husband because marrying him was her choice. But that's what we do too. For some reason we equate suffering to perseverance and misinterpret the gravity of shame, the duration of its presence; how we always end up stuck in the ages it starts.

THE YOUNGER MEN WEREN'T NO better. Granny married both. When her second husband moved in, he was so young her kids couldn't care for him. Him being fifteen years younger than Granny didn't stop him from mustering up his drug-induced courage to swing on her too—but by then, L.A. nem felt bout old as they stepdaddy, so they jumped him. Granny helped and grabbed a knife, but as she brought it down—she missed—and instead inserted the blade into L.A.'s left hand, which had been swinging toward his face. The scar still glistens today.

Both of Granny's husbands—no matter the age or pedigree—couldn't keep they hands to themselves no matter what, even if the what was nothing. Even if all she did was clean they dirty drawls. All she did was clean somebody's dirty drawls, cleaning up after white folk's filth for over thirty years. She worked long hours but would still send the kids to church every Sunday, where they sat until the pastor announced what he would be preaching on, and then they would sneak out the back; scripture embedded somewhere between the four of them. Eventually, cleaning up at home and cleaning up at work took a toll on her body. All that bending over backward trying to keep food on the table—

feeding the kids beets and beans and beating them

heads under mattresses, nobody's heads above water—broke her hip, literally. It happened well into her adult life, early fifties still looking like a brick house. She hadn't made a dent past survival. Never learning how to drive, never granted the time to think about what it was she was good at let alone being able to pursue it. This breaking sat her down flat, sending her straight into retirement. But even now, she still don't know stillness; finding dishes to wash, beds to make, food to cook. Her kids already grown with kids who had kids who had kids and all she got was a JCPenney card, great-grandchildren, her God, and the gout by the age of fifty-five. They put the young one out of they house and back on the block after that one fight though. Only they daddy get dibs at disrespecting they mama.

NEVERLAND

IT TAKES ME TEN MINUTES in the car to write twenty years' worth of feelings down. He tells me doing so will allow me to think about it in a deeper, more emotionally connected way. That it feels like I'm refusing

to take it as seriously as it is. I don't know what any of these words—*deeper, emotionally,* or *connected* mean. I be forgetting I'm supposed to be—pretending to be—a writer—even though I'm more concerned with being a writer than I am with not being depressed. But I take the letter assignment seriously because the only thing I truly know how to be is a student.

As I read what I wrote aloud to him, I try real hard not to focus on how it could read better if I moved this or that sentence around, or changed the first line to something better suited that immediately catches the reader's attention, or amped up the repetition because most things that feel good are about rhythm. I try real hard not to refer to him as the reader, and instead say I think I've always been kinda visibly vacant. How I had a friend tell me once I look dead. How I don't really think sadness or happiness matters in the grand scheme of things, so I never really dwelled on the empty, always unfulfilled accuracy of it all. How I never saw these default states as complete things since I've always known how to laugh, how to smile, how to get things done. How to move on. I don't care about maintaining nothing though. How I don't think I even respect love. That love won't let me let anything I want in for extended periods of time and I don't wanna be like that. Not no more anyways. How every time I've tried to confront it, I would leave more confused and closed off. How I've always had someone on the other end of a conversation tryna convince me what I saw/who I am/what I heard wasn't as fluid as I remember. Which is prolly why I never said nothing about Never. I ain't wanna say sum just to have somebody be like *Kendra, what you talking bout? You ain't never spent the night over there a day in yo life.*

HE FOLDS HIS COPY OF my letter up neatly before placing it in his folder.

"You didn't make it up."

"What?"

"You didn't dream it. It happened. And you should trust yourself more." He tells me I'm not a liar, a maker-upper, or losing my mind, but I do need to find better ways of dealing with depression besides eating edibles and drinking too much NyQuil and deflecting.

"I need it to sleep," I say, although I never sleep. I don't respond to the rest of it.

"Are you okay?" he asks, and I nod. Really, I feel like I'm wasting both of our time by continuing to talk about the same thing every single week, but I can't stop. I say something stupid about the answer, the naming I've been begging him for and he asks me why do I make it a habit to categorize and compare sufferings. He asks me if what happened, happened to anybody else—let alone them having to be in such proximity to the person who did it their entire life on top of other types of disturbances simultaneously happening around them—would it be a big deal then?

"Yeah." I quiet down my stupid.   start back . . .

I tell him people come to me all the time with this type of stuff and I don't know why. So many people. So many mothers. So many girls who sit on my bed and spill, and how I'm ready to move on their behalf yet offer them none of me in return. Not because I can't, but I genuinely never thought it was important enough to even be in the conversation; how if the molestation didn't happen, I'd prolly still be here depressed because that's just how I am.

"You the first person I ever told this stuff to." I shut up. I've heard myself say this to him a lot. It's a script that's starting to piss me off. It sound so stupid when I start to think about the gravity of all those other girls; because I don't wanna think of myself as that girl.

"It ain't like I was raped."

I'm too far gone. I think I'm tryna get kicked outta therapy.

"Plus, Never done did way worse things to me [indirectly] than this." I admit. "This on the bottom of the list of things I resent him for," I try to convince somebody, but it's too unbelievable to not be called pitiful. He starts unfolding my letter again where I mention if Never died, I'd feel mixed emotions about it because although I'd be sad, I've also fantasized about making him bleed and using his blood to write out how I did it.

"Is what you just said about having a list of more severe things actually true, or did you only deflect because you find the worst thing he's ever done to you too shame-filled to admit?"

I hate therapy.

"I mean, yea, cause so much other stuff falls from it. I think about it every blue moon. It'll be in some random places too. I'll be out eating. Or driving. Or laying down, and all of a sudden it'll hit me, like *Damn, that really happened*." How I don't remember it
   until I keep remembering it.

The first time I do, I turn ten; get my hair braided up into a too-tight ponytail; & I cry for hours over the headache. & my brain hurts for days. & I wear brown construction worker boots on purpose. & my friends keep calling 'em concrete busters. & seven of 'em come to a weekend-long sleepover L.A. hosts at my uncle's house. & my best friend is beautiful & her and Never remind me of one another, both hard to miss; how they both can be a lot even though I love them. How I watch them pick at each other throughout the night, and my chest starts to beat real hard all of a sudden once I notice. Not because my birthday party is now about her beauty, but because facing windows are flooding my membrane. How up until then, the sensation of the memory had been idle. But my eyes get closed, again. I'm awakened outta my sleep, again.

My hand is being cradled and held and choreographed, again. How I THINK I'M DREAMING.

"My body started burning like it do whenever I gotta give blood and somebody gotta remind me this is my party but all night, all I wanna do is tell L.A. that she needs to take my friend back home. I can't think about nothing else." I make sure Never is never in a room alone with her. How I think I'm handling what happened with me well, considering how I made myself forget it happened, but wouldn't be able to stand by and watch it happen to anyone else. How I don't even know what to call it, nor do I really know who it is I'm trying to protect. How all the fun I was having halts.

"Now that I just said that I think maybe it's the reason I don't take my birthdays that seriously." How I'm not that big on celebrating myself, just repeating myself. How I'm the best gift giver tho, because I listen.

"What's crazy is after that, it literally never comes to mind when I actually see Never. It's always random. Like when I'm actually having a good time. But I never cry about it. Not even once."

"Do you wanna cry about it?"

"Iono man. I just think it's kinda weird that I don't cry about nothing unless I get real mad or like . . . I'm watching *America's Next Top Model* or sum."

"Huh? *America's Next Top Model* makes you cry?"

"Like seeing people reach they goals be making me cry sometimes. That's what I mean."

"Gotcha. Gotcha. Do you think that's why you put so much of your worth into your work?"

"Prolly. I mean being good at stuff . . . winning stuff . . . always feels . . . iono. People talk to me about stuff I'm good at more than they talk to me. Like they waiting on me to solve a riddle or sum. I don't know what I'm tryna say but since I was a kid, I saw people see me the more and more I tried. So I wasn't scared to fail or embarrass myself in physical form. I wasn't scared to put myself out there creatively. That eventually I get past the failure if I keep practicing and if I don't get good—I at least get competent. So that's the only way people get to know me. That's how I made friends. Or how I became captain of teams. And even how I was able to forget. Which is my fault too because that's the energy I be giving off. That I care about accomplishment and I'm cool with being lonely because I've always felt that way. Always, except for when I'm moving or making. It's hard until it's not as hard. Then they start tryna downplay it like it's been an easy thing to do; like it took nothing, like it comes naturally for me. So then all this attention to getting good is also how I've lost friends and quit teams and have the same conversations over and over. Which is why I'm just kinda the way I am now. Writing been the exact same way for me except now, although I wanna accomplish things within it, I don't wanna make it my whole personality, my whole life. I would actually love to start having a life outside of constantly tryna achieve if I'm being forreal. I just don't know how because then ima have to be a person . . . in front of other people . . . like all the time."

REDMAN AVE

L.A. FOLLOWS ME OUT OF her room and asks Never to get up to do something like take out the trash or clean up his shit all over the house, except Never don't move. Not even a lil bit. Not even as she says it for the second time. When he don't move the third time, I already know he was probably listening to our conversation in the room where L.A. just told me he done stole money out of her purse. She ask me not to bring it up, but pay attention. I simply don't care enough to do either, but I do ask if she's sure since she got a habit of accusing folk of stealing things she's often misplaced. Never extremely smart and by extremely smart I mean extremely calculated, so it's hard to think he careless enough to steal outta something that sits in the same spot every single day. L.A. say this ain't the first thing that done came up missing. Portable DVD players, other small amounts of money, etc., etc., etc. She just ain't say nothing.

"Never, I'm already this much off you," L.A. say.

Being "this much off you" is a warning. I know the tone, so I turn my head around to look out the kitchen and into the living room to see her pinching her fingers into a flat surface to accentuate the *this* in her statement. The *this* is the fist-sized hole in L.A.'s living room wall he made while the girl he was sneaking out of windows for was over without permission and his lie being a plumber L.A. didn't order being the culprit. See, stuff.

Everything has a backstory.

"So you might wanna get up and do what I said," she finishes.

At this point, I'm bout ready to get up and do what she said cause I know she finna start swinging soon. Threatening violence is not a threat, it's just something that's gone happen the longer you take. & like a guilty person, Never hop up from the floor with an urgency that would have immediately got me knocked back down on it. Or at least a hit to the chest, which is why I think they ain't growing. Let me steal a Skittle and I'm getting drop-kicked, back bent, and bruised up. Let me say no twice, and I might not have no bones when I wake up. Never, on the other hand, starts talking loud and getting in L.A.'s face—which is really something I ain't never seen nobody do in my entire life except for his mama.

Me and mine notice how his body swells over hers—not because he got caught, but because he can't believe she got the nerve to confront him about it. Niggas be weird that way too. They never be mad about what they did. They just be mad you reminding them they did it.

"Oh! You think I stole yo money!" is the first thing Never say once he's on his feet, which lets us know he definitely did that shit even though we already knew he did that shit. I know he prolly was standing outside of the door listening to our conversation. He do shit like that too, creep around looking for information to use against you at a later date.

Everything gets real still in this house I didn't wanna live in. At first I thought he was stealing for girls, but then I thought about how any reason is null since L.A. would give him anything if he asked. So I assume Never is finna die cause L.A. has always made it clear to me that: *Whenever you feel like you ready to fight me, you betta come hard, cause it's gone be the last time you put yo hands on anybody.* But all she say is:

"You not finna be living here and stealing my money," way more calmly than I thought she would, like she want him to pick between the two; like giving him a choice is the only thing she cares about. So she tells him again, to go and do what she asked him to.

But he won't. Then all she say is:

"Kendra, go get a belt."

I ain't sure why she decides to take the belt route with this sixteen-year-old instead of using one of her army hand-breaking moves on him. Maybe she instructs me to go get a belt because deep down, she really don't wanna hurt him; he's her favorite boy, and having to hurt him will hurt her, and this hesitation makes me think for the first time ever that maybe hitting a child is wrong; since up until now, I been the only child getting hit. Whatever the reason, I don't remember how she gets a belt in her hand, because I don't move either. But it's there, and she got a good grip on it, cause when she swing it down, I hear the wind whine.

I **MOVE OUT OF THE** kitchen into the living room as L.A. slings the belt across Never's body like she's in danger. He laughing though, which lets me know this ain't no normal whooping; that this a *I ain't little no more* moment desperate for revenge—on both of their parts. L.A. ain't nine no mo', and Never ain't gone go where he's told to go no mo'. And I get scared.

Me running away from them both is a statement. The closer they get to me, the more I try to get away. I rush into L.A.'s room and let the doorway frame my eleven-, twelve-, maybe ten-year-old body. I stand there—still, stunned, like every girl in every horror movie I've ever closed my eyes through, and I start screaming like a person who wants the killer the find them. I don't desire power over nobody, barely even myself.

L.A. swings the belt again as they migrate into the hallway that stretches from the tip of the living room—across all our bedrooms—and all the way to the garage door. He pushing L.A. off of him, not necessarily trying to take the belt out of her hand, but holding her wrist in order to steady it and gain control over where it goes. They ignore me even as they pass me. Never get a tighter grip on the leather—which halts L.A's form as he jerks it forward—but she got military strength and survivor instinct so she don't fall.

She pulls up and back to get enough room to swing the belt back across his legs as they fall deeper into the hallway, past my room door of this house that she loves. That she's so proud of. How as her husband I'm supposed to help protect her, but here I am letting it crumble. In less than two years, it'll get foreclosed, and I'll be content with moving back into an apartment, to a more closeted space. I won't consider how defeated L.A. feels about her house being gone until she keeps making it a point to drive by it for no reason sometimes to see who's inside—to wonder how they might've changed the wood floors in the kitchen to tile because they couldn't comprehend the vision.

But right now the vision is me standing; still unable to move, but begging for them to please stop. That's what I scream— "Mama, stop!!!!!" I'm useless. My brain keeps telling me to jump in, but my body won't move. It's too scared to touch anyone's body again. But I'm not aware of this yet. It's too many other factors to focus on. I don't know whose side I'm supposed to be on—the child, or the mother. My hands are too scared to touch anyone's body again. Never's body especially. I wish I were aware of it. I don't know whose side I'm supposed to be on. I equate me not moving to when my English teacher tells L.A. "Kendra is . . . passive." During a parent-teacher conference. I ain't know what the word meant, but I knew it sounded negative. Bad. Like a word I never wanted to be associated with, ever. But I am, and it makes me

an even more apparent statue, a willing participant in either letting all the women around me die, or letting all the children around me suffer, all because I'm afraid of my palms.

By the time they get to Never's room door, the walls are only wiggly lines through my tears. Like this is now a fun house. And I keep hearing him laughing as L.A. gives the best beating her arms can manage. I feel like if they get to the back door, I'll run out of air. I don't know what to do

with my hands. My mouth has always been my best asset. I don't know what to do with my hands. I don't even wanna bite them. I run to L.A.'s bed and grab her cell phone off the charger to find my uncle's number because he's the only man I know and they say that's who you supposed to call when shit like this happens. It's not that I think he'll do anything. If L.A. wasn't actually involved, I would be calling her same way everybody else do. But it's not an option right now. And through hiccup tears and a heaving chest and the commotion still happening in the background, I scramble up my sentences into phrases, "You gotta come get Never . . . him and . . . him and my mama fighting . . . please . . . come now." I'm losing it. Hysterical. Having the breakdown I wish I was brave enough to replicate. I don't remember ever crying so hard in my life. Ever. Instead of him being on the way without question like I know L.A. would, he asks, "What you mean by 'fighting'?"

& I power off.

Weeks later when life is back to normal and we at my uncle's house sitting around reenacting it all, they laugh at me. Crack up and say "Kendra called us crying and we ain't know what she was saying she was crying so hard."

"Ain't nobody bout to be all up in my mama face," I'm told.

"Why you let him do that?" I'm asked.

& I power off. For good.

I don't know what I expect by calling, seeing as how Never got kicked out and into our house for doing way less. They ain't want him, that's why he here. But my uncle asking mad irrelevant questions like Never some kinda criminal he gotta prepare for or we gotta get rid of, and not just a kid, is not what I thought would happen at all. I wipe snot away and I don't even think the word *police*—let alone calling them; but he mentions it, and quickly. I hang up the phone and run back to stand in the doorway.

"You tired, ain't you?" Never ask L.A. at some point and continues to laugh in her face, which makes her laugh later—her shoulders floating up and down as she remembers "I was tired denna mug." But in the moment, him asking her this makes her madder so she keeps swinging and running outta breath tryna whoop the gall out. It don't work. It's not supposed to.

Never not reacting or bursting into tears only pisses a Black mama off further, so I can't believe it when she gives up. They don't make it to the back door, but she tells him he gotta go in the morning in the exact same fashion Never uses when he kicks L.A. out in the middle of the night years later. How she drives us nine hours to Colorado snow to go see him then. How by this time he done started his own family, got his own spot, and finally feels man enough. How he's been waiting his whole life for the moment. How it's all very predictable seeing as how I predicted it. How he still listening behind doors in his own house. How seeing it happen twice is how I finally come to understand he's never actually ever been asleep, only pretending. How he probably waited outside of bathroom doors in the morning time. How this ain't no different. How him and L.A. start screaming random things at each other this time too. How they get closer and closer the more that is said—chest to chest. How YOU AIN'T NOBODY! How YOU CAN GET THE FUCK OUT! How GET YO SHIT! How YOU AIN'T NEVER DONE SHIT! How AIN'T NOBODY ASK YOU TO COME HERE! How YOU DON'T RUN SHIT UP IN HERE! How THIS MY HOUSE! How I'm eleven and seven at once. How I'm so tired of using the world *again*. How I hate love, I hate love. I hate love. I can't feel it. How L.A. spends days buying Never housewarming gifts and overextending herself and cooking for him and and and and and and and. How Never kicks her outta his house in the middle of a cold, cold night before Christmas. How there's witnesses this time. How still nobody defends L.A. Again. Not even me. How I'm still too busy crying on couches with my hands under my thighs and my music loud. How Never justifies his plotting and says it's in defense of his own mother. How L.A. is the one who drove his mother here to be with him. How they always turn on her until they need her, or a place to stay, or some food to eat, or to mother their children, or some gas money, or a ride. How I tell her this all the time and she never listens. How she tells me if they using her then that mean I'm using her too. How she always forgiving folk who laughs in her face about the way they treat her. How they know she gone take them back. How maybe I'm also a mother. How I can't forgive nobody. How I think I kinda hate them all and if I allow myself to feel it, I'm scared of what I might make. How when it happens this time, I walk out the door with L.A. through the palm soft winter snow. How we only ever get ice down here. How I'm asking if she aight because I don't know how to say sorry for sitting instead of killing. How I think maybe our relationship is my issue. How being a child has never felt like an excuse to me with so much responsibility between us. How I can't save her when she can't see. How the first thing she do when we get to the car is call back home. How nowhere I've ever been has felt like it. How they all ask "Ain't ya'll supposed to be staying all week?" and it's been two days. How L.A. tells them what happened as she turns the heater up on full blast. How I don't know how nobody willingly live in this weather; thawing out the body shouldn't be such a process. How I start to lay my seat back to relax when L.A. stops me, tells me to go inside. How I feel like I made it obvious I wanna be with her, being in the car and all, but I say it anyways, "I wanna stay with you."

"Kendra, go back in," she say.

"Why I gotta go back in there. I don't wanna be in there with them. When we leaving? Why we can't just leave? Mama, can we please leave? I can drive." How I sound like a baby even though I'm sixteen. Or six. I say it all in one breath. How I'm so angry at her that I ask to stay by her side. How I'm too disappointed in both of us to care if she needs to be alone.

"We can't leave right now. It's too late and I don't know how to drive in snow at night. We'll leave in the morning." How she ain't know how to drive in snow in the day either, yet here we are. How I didn't get a choice in whether or not I wanted to be here in the first place. How I look around the car.

"Where you gone sleep then? In here?"

"Yeah. I'll be alright," she say. "Gone back in and don't start nothing, Kendra." How I don't know why she say this to me since the only thing I care about starting is a countdown to when I can age out of family.

. . .

But the night L.A. tries to beat Never blacker than blue with that belt—when she's done, she don't push me away— she comes back to her doorway where I'm at. Says it's all alright. That she all right. That it's all over. It's all good. That she gotta find somewhere to take him, but it's late and she'll figure it out in the morning.

Never leave out the back door the same night; and by the time my uncle pulls up—the police is returning Never in the back seat.

Outside, we all stand around the cop car, and my face feels like my hands did that morning I scrubbed them too long. Wrinkly and raw in the wind as the cops address my uncle even though this L.A. house. Say they found Never walking down the freeway and since we live so far out, Never—black as every night in a technically colorless place—was picked right on up; that big-ass white shirt probably giving him away. If he ain't have it on, he probably coulda faded into the sky.

The cops say to Never at least fifteen times each, "When you turn seventeen, you can do whatever you want."

When you turn seventeen, you can leave
When you turn seventeen, you can go

When you turn seventeen, you can walk up and down the
  street and not have a home
When you turn seventeen, you don't have to stay here
When you turn seventeen . . .
In Texas, when you turn seventeen, you considered an adult
How long you got 'til you seventeen?

THEY SAY IT SO MANY times it feel like an operation, and because Never ain't got nowhere else to go—he take his sixteen-year-old ass back in the house. Into his very own room. And L.A. lets it all go like that. She don't push the issue. By the morning, she done prayed on it and forgave before waking us to get ready for church.

Then Never locks himself in the bathroom for hours blasting the same song I used to love on repeat.

And L.A. bangs on the door the entire time.

It's all so tiring. All so stupid. I don't ever wanna be in love.

I sit on the floor with my back against the couch in full church garb—stockings included. I swallow every fingernail I can manage with my dog's chin in my lap and my heart clapping outta my chest.

FIRST DAY OUT

ON MY FIRST DAY OF high school I become a cliché and have a panic attack that I'm forced to admit is happening since it lasts an entire semester. I stand at the door of a cafeteria with hundreds of long, busy lunch tables where I don't know a single person. And even though the days of wanting to maintain any interpersonal relationship I've ever had, or even establish any new ones, feel way past me, I don't make it two steps across the threshold before my chest starts doing the thing chests do when your blood wants relief. I only know I'm panicking because my insides feel like when I take too many puffs of my albuterol. My sternum gets all jittery like there's too many breaths to catch simultaneously, or I keep missing all the breaths in the air I'm supposed to be catching. 1. I realize having to make a decision about where to sit seems impossible. 2. I begged L.A. to let me come to this school. 3. There is no number three. There's just me. It's always gone be just me, hoping to vanish in a way that is everlasting and uncomplicated.

Emotionally—even the panic is kinda underwhelming if I'm being honest. It all feels like my best days. It all feels like my worst days. It's still not the complete breakdown of violence and vitriol I'm waiting for; that I think is required for folk to finally leave me alone for the rest of my life, but it's enough to make me backpedal out of the cafeteria.

There's so many people in these halls at all times since my school is a mini college campus where literally thousands upon thousands of students flood all the spaces as if we're an ant pile that's been stepped on. It takes forever to get back up a hallway, to migrate through the concert crowds constantly coming around every crevice of every corner. I hear all the voices of all the people surrounding me but can't make words out of the sounds. It's all static. It's all a riot. The main building is three floors and I get lost in it and get lost trying to get out of it. I try to remember why I wanted to go here when all my friends I went to school with my whole life went somewhere else. I try to figure out why I make it a point to isolate myself. I've always had an urge to leave, to be gone, to go away to a place where nobody can see me and nobody can know me and nobody can touch me. I still do. I get this about myself now. It don't matter where. A closet. A bathroom. Anything that locks is sufficient.

As my body reject my brain—or as my brain reject my body—I find a restroom on the west wing of the building that's far enough away from the class I gotta return to after lunch, but also close enough to class where I won't be late. I stay here, in this restroom, hoping none of my classmates come in and recognize my shoes. Sometimes if other kids come in to stand around the sink to talk or reapply makeup for too long, I'll flush the toilet with my sneaker every couple minutes until they leave. I rather them think I'm shitting than have them know I'm scared. I stay here, in this restroom, the duration of the semester. It becomes my favorite hiding spot because it's small with only two stalls. I stand in it reading books that weren't assigned. Eventually, it backfires and I start failing multiple classes and end up in summer school because I can't concentrate long enough to grasp any of the lessons because I'm so nervous all the time and can't figure out why

this feeling has decided to consume me out of nowhere when I don't even know its name or what it wants, but it keeps screaming in my ear to flee.

The stall is gross, but the capacity of its close confines make me feel safe, close to something, and most importantly—it calms me down. This is before I learn where the school library is and that it's there for students like me in moments like this and before I eventually make friends with people who are like the other side of me, the ones I let them see; but while I'm hiding, somedays I learn that there's others around who share its confines with me. Who are like me, and who can't move either. How we lock ourselves inside in order to get away. How I latch my backpack onto the keyhole on the back of the door so grabbing the book I meticulously placed in last to grab first is easier. How if there's no book to read, I'll put in my headphones and turn the volume to a level where it can't be heard from the outside. How if I don't got no music, I'll recite song lyrics to myself while locking and unlocking my knees to the beat until the bell rings. How on a good day, I do all three at once. How on a bad day, I spend the time figuring out what lie to tell when L.A. asks me what I ate today. How on all the days, I wonder if who I am this day—is who I'll always be from here on out.

NEVERLAND

WHEN I SAY I TOLD L.A., he closes the folder again; puts his pen down. I fix myself to sit as straight as him, use my elbows to push my slouching spine off the couch and into attention.

"Really," he answers. "And how did that go?"

"Well," I start, I change my mind, rest my elbows on my knees. Because I'm big on setting the scene, I say, "First I asked her to come walk my dog with me."

He nods. I always knew the first sentence is everything.

"Then I asked her not to let what I'm finna tell her affect her own personal relationships to said people or make what I'm finna tell her about herself or her ability to safely parent, cause you know she got the tendency to do so." & he nods again, assures me that was a good thing to do.

"Then I told her the same thing I told you."

"And?"

"And then she kept asking me if he touched me. Like him touching me is the only real thing that could matter. And I got confused again, and thought maybe I misinterpreted the situation seeing as how we was both kids and kids be curious."

He picks back up the pen, but notes ain't necessary at this point, because ain't nothing to unpack since I never thought telling her woulda changed nothing. How Never prolly still would've lived with us all them times because she still wanted to save him, be close to him, and although she can say—and have said—this wouldn't have been the outcome, I don't see it being no other way. That yeah, it would've been confrontation for sure, but no resolve, no real boundary, but I finish my story anyway because finishing my story is the only thing I care about.

"Then, tell me why when she went back home—the very next weekend—she post a picture at a birthday dinner with her standing right next to him. Hand on his shoulder. Allat. Smiling. So yeah, like I said—it don't matter, cause when I brought it up to her she said I asked her not to tell nobody and told her not to let it affect her relationship to him."

He nods again, says something about that kid thing not being an excuse on Never's behalf, again; and asks me about the rest of L.A.'s Christmas break visit.

"Maaaaaaaan I only told her cause you told me I should think about it." I hate letting someone help me. "But I had already thought about it. For decades. But decided I wouldn't, cause like I said"—I clap each syllable out for him—"IT. DO. NOT. MATTER. BRO. But I'm tryna do better. I'm tryna be a different person. I'm trying to wanna have fuller relationships with the people who love me. So the day before I do tell her, we at Jason's Deli right, waiting on our food cause I love Jason's Deli. I tell you I used to work there? Anyways, we standing in the middle of Jason's Deli right, and I already got an attitude because she showed up to my apartment with another person I asked her not to bring to my apartment for similar reasons. Now if I said noun one of them could stay after driving nine hours—I'd be wrong. But she brought the kids along and knew I wasn't gone turn them away, so now I'm extra pissed cause it's literally the same story twenty years later. It's just a new set of kids. And I get even more mad cause she try to make it like my problem is she wanna take care of people's kids. It's literally never about the kids. It be bout them kids' parents and her. And it's fucked up that a new batch of kids is finna be exposed to the same shit because don't nobody wanna tell the truth about how they don't care enough to try to do things differently for the kids they claim to care so much about. I say this all the time, but they act like I'm the one trippin' because I don't say it nicely. But like you said, I can only change myself. I gotta let it go." I barely take a breath.

"Anyways, we standing in the lil waiting area of Jason's Deli right, and I'm giving short answers to her questions cause it's a lot going on. It's a lot of people around. I don't really wanna talk cause I feel like she asking so many questions cause she know she wrong for the pop up stunt she just pulled." I roll my wrists. "But she keep going. She keep going. She keep going. She don't stop. And I'm not saying nothing bro cause I ain't tryna hurt her feelings. And I ain't tryna do it in front of these kids. But now I feel like a kid again so it's even harder. So all I say is *I don't wanna talk*. That's all I say." I inhale real deep and start talking with my hands again.

"Tell me why this lady start praying over me. Like real life puts her hands on me—over my head in the middle of Jason's Deli bro, and starts to pray aloud; talking bout I got a 'spirit' on me that's making me hard to be around, whispering shit about anxiety and depression and tolerance and how I'm moody and irritable and asking God for my patience and my mind."

He don't start writing, just keeps nodding, cause clearly—I'm never done.

"So I ended up telling her the next morning cause I thought maybe all the shit we been talking bout in here all these months was boiling over. I been having a hard time, the worst time of my life tryna accept that all this shit even happened to me that I can't even talk about it as if it happened to me; I talk about it like

I just happened to be there. I mean, you know, you the one who pointed it out. I can't do it. I don't know how to do it. But I'm glad I am doing it. But yea, I just don't want my first instinct to be to leave. Cause like, I'll leave you bro. Even if I love you to death. And be good if we never speak again in life."

I don't really know what I'm talking bout no more, but I keep going.

"Then I feel crazy because the people I'm mad at done been through waaaay more than me; but that's a trick my family done played on me too. They act like because I didn't go through what they went through, that it's not that deep. And that's the way I started moving from real young. I internalized it; like whatever happens . . . get over it. Or go to practice. Or do something. Like it's so much shit. I spent a lot of time blaming myself for having the time to remember. I literally thought because my hand was holding Never's penis that I was the one in the wrong. Like I was the one who did something to him. Same way I blamed myself for not protecting my mama from him. Same way I blamed myself for not protecting my mama from my daddy. Same way I couldn't hold my mama accountable for none of it because I felt sorry for her same way she felt sorry for them. And I don't want nobody feeling sorry for me so I act like ain't nothing ever that big of a deal. And now it's biting me in the ass cause I gotta unlearn it. That's why I be so high." I throw my back against the couch. "I'm high right now." I wanna sit on the floor so bad. "My bad.

"But yea, anyways, what L.A. said wasn't all the way a lie. I mean, none of it was really. I been hard to be around because I don't wanna be around. I am easily annoyed, which I never really showed until I was like . . . seventeen. When I turned seventeen, maybe eighteen. Yea, I think it was when I left for Chicago. Up until then I was just enduring and laughing through it and being funny Kendra who had an exciting childhood and this super-rare bond with her mama. And that's all true. All the way true. But it's a lot of other things that's true too and it all equally contributed. It be feeling like niggas never want me to be nothing else but a site of . . ." I really don't have a word to explain what I feel. "Sum. I don't know. Joy? Like these people really think I'm a happy person bro. & that's my fault because I really tried to be." I get back to the point. "Like I said, when I told her, she kept asking me was I sure Never didn't touch me. She asked me like ten times and the more I heard the question, the more it felt like she was implying it was just a penis. Which is the exact same thing I been saying to you. Then I asked her why do it matter if he touched me or not when I just told you that nigga put his penis in my hand—which is exactly what you been saying to me."

Then he starts writing again.

"What did she say when you said this?"

"Started getting loud, voice started cracking, talking bout how whether or not I got touched mattered a whole lot." I shrug my shoulder. "I guess my hands ain't apart of my body."

CRASH DUMMIES

L.A. TELLS ME NEVER IS staying with us again.

"For a couple of weeks," she say. But I can already tell he been there longer since she only telling me cause summer's ending. "It's good you coming home tho," she add, "so you can get the car."

I'm getting ready to start my senior year. I'm quiet, seeing as how two weeks after I get the car Doll promised me for two years—I crash it in the rain rushing to school. The hood pops open like it's jack-in-the-box, slamming into my windshield after a car in front of me hesitates at the stoplight. I hit it—which in turn makes the F-150 that's on my tail hit me; & glass bursts into my lap and my blood starts to flow. I pull shards out of the seats, my thighs, and my hands. I spend weeks with a chiropractor. I got the guts from cuts spilling out every second & all summer, all Doll do is tell me about how the accident skyrocketed his insurance. He don't ask am I ok once, but goes on and on every other day about how the woman I hit sued him. How he can't believe I'm so careless. How he knows the accident was my fault cause I don't pay attention. How he not paying to get the car fixed. Which is fine; since L.A. already got it fixed. But once she do, everything else on it begins to break down quickly. The engine stalls out at stoplights and the brakes are almost nonexistent. So I make an executive decision to leave it be. I park it in the garage of our apartment in Garland, throw the keys in the drawer, finish the school year on the school bus, and spend one of my last summers in Houston. All of which is why I'm confused as L.A. informs me how the car that's supposed to be parked broke down again and is now sitting at some corner store up the street, so I ask.

"Never was driving it." She say it like I'm dumb for not connecting the dots.

"Why was he driving my car?" I try to ask with the most genuine tone I can muster because I don't got the energy to argue with L.A. about no borders or no Never or nobody else no more really.

"He needed to go somewhere and ain't no bus route over here."

"Okay . . ." I feel myself start to scale, but my throat is closing up so it sounds like I'm whining, "And what that got to do with him driving my car?" I start back. Never is grown now and I would never let a grown-ass man who can get a car use mine to ride around doing nothing in. "Why would you be letting him ride around in my car? I don't get that. Like I don't get what you saying. It ain't really making sense."

"Kendra"—her voice is already up four more octaves than it was before. "I ain't gotta explain nothing to you." I'm waiting for her to mention how she the one who got the car fixed in the first place, or whatever else to remind me I don't got a right to question her bout nothing when she's the one who been doing everything for me my whole life. I'm too unbalanced to realize it's never not been implied. "He was driving the car cause I said he could and it broke down like it usually do."

"Why is it still up there? You just wasn't gone say nothing until I got home? Why ain't nobody went and got it yet," I say more than ask.

"It's not my car. I don't know. Never said it won't start at all." Which means she probably drove up there to get him.

"Okay, so what I'm supposed to do?" I need a concrete answer to this question that don't involve me having to ask Doll for help or tell him what's going on. Him giving me this car makes him believe he's had a heavy hand in my upbringing and I should hold it up as an undying symbol of my gratitude toward him and never ask him for anything ever again although whatever I have ever asked him for—somebody had to make me do it.

"Tell ya daddy to come and get it I guess." She say, "I don't know."

...

"You *been* letting him use the car." Doll say when I sum up my phone call in two sentences. "Don't lie."

"What?" The stuff he be saying sometimes bro. I just don't get it. It's no point in engaging. He don't believe me, since he don't really know me. Everybody acting like my car being infiltrated without my consent is secondary to the situation kinda got me in a trance.

"Never just happen to be riding around in yo car for weeks and you ain't know?" I roll all my eyes.

"We don't really be talking like that so I'ma say nah," I say, and ask him to refer back to the conversation we had five minutes ago where I told him what I was told.

"I'ma go get the car, but I'ma bringing it back here." Doll say. I really wanna be like *Okay . . . and . . . this shit hot as hell anyways*. And I love having a car, even if it ain't got no air-conditioning; but if it mean I don't gotta talk to him about it no more, I can handle not having it.

He tell me we leaving right now instead of next week like we planned to and it's like everything these niggas do is always about finding ways to punish you. I get up and pack my shit and hop in the truck. I'm tired. Of him and her and them. & Doll talk nonstop for three hours straight. Saying everything he already said about the car—in the car. How it's my responsibility and I'm supposed to know who's in it at all times and how he ain't give it to me to let niggas be riding round in it and how I'm sneaky because he ain't even know about it getting fixed in the first place and why do I lie to him so much and whatever else until we pull up to the apartment.

I text Never we downstairs cause he the only one who know where the car at.

I say "Hey."

He say "Hey" back, followed by a "What's up!" with a smile on his face since him and Doll ain't seen each other in a long time; and all the shit I had to listen to for the past few hours go out of the window. Ain't no scowling, no accusations, no nothing. Doll's frown turns right side up. It ain't no interrogation. No follow-up question. No nothing as Never explain how he went to the store for some gars and the car wouldn't start back. It's probably the truth and a lie but I don't care.

"Yeah, them cars, man, they do that. Especially after you bang it up like she did." Doll say after Never tells him the same thing I told him L.A. told me. And that's that. They don't even dwell on it. Just start reminiscing.

DOLL SAY SOMETHING ABOUT REMEMBERING taking Never to the pool to teach him how to swim when he was a little boy while

I remember Never taking me to the pool when I was a little girl and almost drowning. How Never laughed at my flailing but I didn't know my father taught him everything he knew. Doll say it's crazy how time go cause Never got his own daughter now. I don't ever want a daughter—who is the only daughter—or the first daughter—or the last. But I'll be damned if I ever have a son.

Never say sum like yea, time goes, but I'm balled up in the corner of the back seat, mostly because I'm cold, only look-ing into the rearview mirror when something outlandish is stated like Doll agreeing with Never that I been like a lil sister and I'm the family's last hope of "doing it"—like the path I'm headed down is glaring back at them. I don't know what's going on but I wish I had a stronger word other than dissociation to describe it.

My heart is being a heart again. I can't believe I'm supposed to believe either of us love each other. I nub my teeth against each finger until I find the one with the most skin left and put it in my mouth and stare out of the window. I don't know what *it* is and why they think whatever *it* is I do will be for them as if recollec-tion don't exist.

Doll looks back at me through the rearview mirror and sees my face, decides now is the time to parent me, to pay attention to me, when I refuse to give mine to him.

"You don't care about the stuff people give you," he starts up, again. And I don't care about the stuff he gives me so I still don't say nothing, just pull back the hanging skin of my thumb until it sits at my knuckle until I feel the pressure of air sting the open wound.

I SLIGHTLY TURN MY HEAD to see him through the slit of the mir-ror. I'm mostly confused as to what it is about Never that makes folk wanna impress him by putting me on display. At least it feels that way. I get paranoid, concerned by what it is they all pretend not to see.

I deny Doll another response like my silence has ever stopped shit from playing out.

"You don't even take care of it," he adds. & I start to hum over him so I won't open up the car door. I put my thumb in my mouth and snatch the hanging skin off with my teeth.

"You just gone sing over what I'm saying? Boy, I tell ya." Doll hangs his head and starts back speaking to Never, "You see how she do me?"

Never mention something about me being a teenager having something do with my disposition but that's the last thing I hear because I'm too busy wondering does Never see it too.

I get too blinded by how the red bubbles up so fast, so easily in the creases.

How all this time all I had to do was bite.

How my throat burns so brightly.

How the flesh endures so willingly, but I don't have to be
    a mother.

How I feel as bare in this car as I did in that bed.

How I think for the first time I might need help.

How I think all of us might need help.

How when L.A. needed help, she fled to war for similar
    reasons.

How her mother doesn't know about her child's reasoning.

How when L.A. got shipped to basic training, she got bunked
    with nothing but men.

How it's so hard for women to fall asleep in sacred spaces.

How Doll's claim kept her safe until it exposed her.

How men only seem to respect other men who own things.

How we all kinda homeless.

How I'm seventeen and close to leveraging it.

How I had to learn cleaning the blood is a science.

How it's so hard to touch my insides twice.

How I take over my mind so nobody got the power to
 kill me.

How I'm not proud of it.

How this don't really matter right now.

How I rock and suck the red coming out of the hole in
 my finger.

How sometimes if I don't clasp my hands above my head
 at night, I won't fall asleep.

ACKNOWLEDGMENTS

I been working real hard on not oversharing as much and this just made me laugh out loud cause no I'm not. I don't know why I even said that, but I never thought I'd finish this book. Anyways, on the very first day of my very first writing workshop, I was freezing in Chicago because I'm from Texas and think layering hoodies is the same as a down coat, when one of the best writing professors I ever had—Kathie Bergquist—had said real casual how "by the time you're thirteen, you have enough to write for a lifetime." I didn't necessarily believe it at first, but I knew the coming-of-age story was always comforting, revisited, and inspiring, and I knew I wanted to write my own, so I kinda needed what she said to be true. Turns out, it's kinda my only true thing. So thank you to all these things, pieces, and people that I returned to and/or thought of often to help remind and encourage me to see it through: The "Keep building it" scene from *The Last Black Man in San Francisco*. Sasha Debevec-McKenney's poem "When I Met Sharon Olds She Told Me to Write a Poem About LBJ's Penis." Isaiah Rashad's music. All of it. *Wounds of Passion* by bell hooks, Alice Walker's story "Coming Apart," all the women across both sides of my family for fighting in whatever way they knew to be effective, and this Sonia Sanchez line: "Now I move in the blood of women who polish pores a capella."

Dr. Cassie Smith, L. Lamar Wilson, and Robin Behn for being my thesis committee and providing direction when I first attempted completing this a few years ago. Nabila Lovelace's *Sons of Achilles* because you already know. Markia, for having the exact same generational cycle breaking talk we have every single time we talk. Denzel Curry's "TABOO | TA13OO." This Hanif Abdurraqib line: "everybody wanna make soul but don't nobody wanna hemorrhage a whole family." And I could stop it right there, but I ain't: "into sweat & white powder & so much sex that they will never speak of what killed you." Sir, please!!! I swear after I read this, it halted my life for months. Marya Spence, Daniel Halpern, Ecco, and every single person involved in getting *Fruit Punch* out into the world, from Gabriella to Sonya, thank ya'll. All the kid characters across all the screens that I found support and laughter and language in while I grew and as I'm growing up, but especially Jordan from *The Bernie Mac Show*, who is a visual representation of me at that age, and, above all else, Eve Batiste in *Eve's Bayou*—the most important, epic movie of my life. I didn't think what I thought inside existed until I saw Eve being what I was. I think about some aspect of it all the time and "You think just cause you got blood in your pants you don't have to act civilized no more?!?" is this book's—and my life's—guiding light. It's kept me dramatically humorous. Vince Staples's short film *Prima Donna*, Edwidge Danticat's short story "Children of the Sea," and *The Carmichael Show*, which I never get tired of. New Orleans 2019. theMIND's *Don't Let It Go to Your Head*, but "Atlas Complex" especially. Mannnnnn, say. A song. Big, big shoutout to Brooklyn, Riley, and Chloe for ya'll's presence, Facetimes, jokes, dancing, and general "Kendra, is you writing yo book again?" constantly prompting me. Ya'll really amazing watching and learning and regurgitating and making up and all that. That's wild. Knowing ya'll will someday grow up and read this is kinda terrifying, but when that time comes, all I can hope is that ya'll still free. Stay yours first. Love ya'll. Thank ya'll. Oak Cliff, Pleasant Grove, Prichard Lane, Cummings Recreational Center, Maynard H. Jackson elementary and middle school (may it rest in peace, truly the best of times), and anybody I've ever shared a long laugh with, thank you. Just, thank you everything. It all works. It all comes together. Eventually.